::studysync®

Reading & Writing Companion

The Civil War

:::studysync®

studysync.com

Send all inquiries to:
BookheadEd Learning, LLC
610 Daniel Young Drive
Sonoma, CA 95476

Cover, ©iStock.com/gkuchera, ©iStock.com/alexey_boldin, ©iStock.com/skegbydave

1 2 3 4 5 6 7 8 9 DOW 20 19 18 17 16 A

G8U4

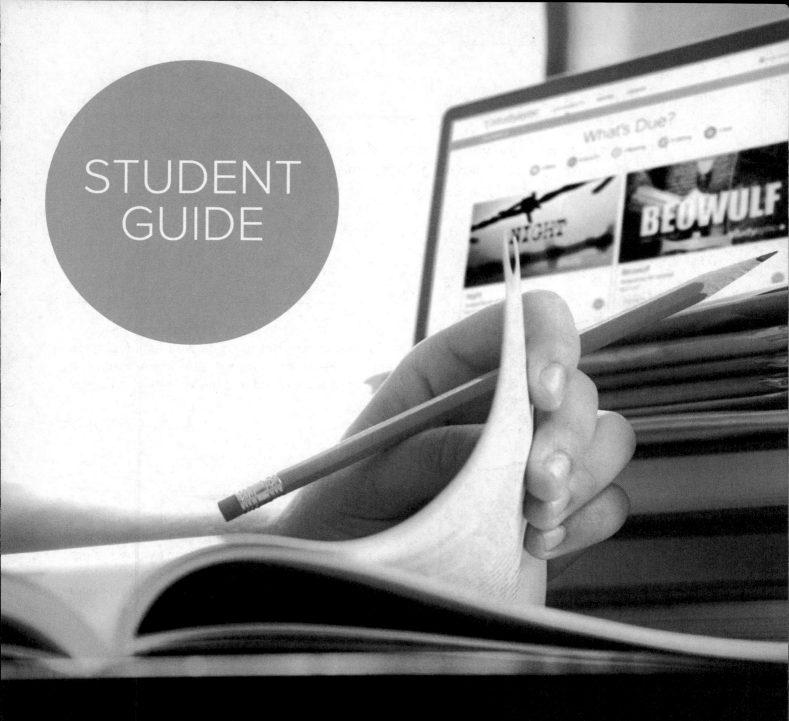

STUDENT GUIDE

GETTING STARTED

Welcome to the StudySync Reading and Writing Companion! In this booklet, you will find a collection of readings based on the theme of the unit you are studying. As you work through the readings, you will be asked to answer questions and perform a variety of tasks designed to help you closely analyze and understand each text selection. Read on for an explanation of each section of this booklet.

CORE ELA TEXTS

In each Core ELA Unit you will read texts and text excerpts that share a common theme, despite their different genres, time periods, and authors. Each reading encourages a closer look with questions and a short writing assignment.

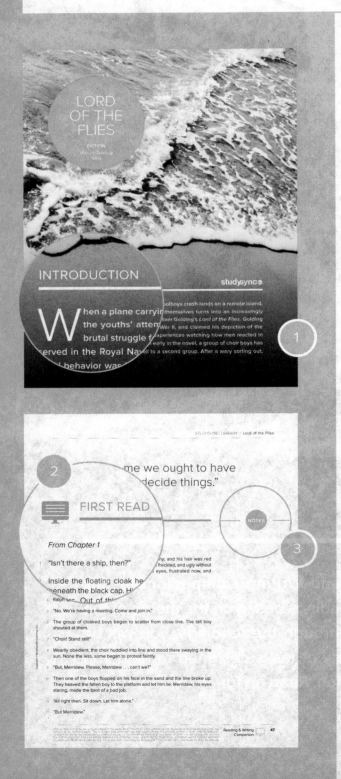

 INTRODUCTION

An Introduction to each text provides historical context for your reading as well as information about the author. You will also learn about the genre of the excerpt and the year in which it was written.

 FIRST READ

During your first reading of each excerpt, you should just try to get a general idea of the content and message of the reading. Don't worry if there are parts you don't understand or words that are unfamiliar to you. You'll have an opportunity later to dive deeper into the text.

 NOTES

Many times, while working through the activities after each text, you will be asked to **annotate** or **make annotations** about what you are reading. This means that you should highlight or underline words in the text and use the "Notes" column to make comments or jot down any questions you may have. You may also want to note any unfamiliar vocabulary words here.

④ THINK QUESTIONS

These questions will ask you to start thinking critically about the text, asking specific questions about its purpose, and making connections to your prior knowledge and reading experiences. To answer these questions, you should go back to the text and draw upon specific evidence that you find there to support your responses. You will also begin to explore some of the more challenging vocabulary words used in the excerpt.

⑤ CLOSE READ & FOCUS QUESTIONS

After you have completed the First Read, you will then be asked to go back and read the excerpt more closely and critically. Before you begin your Close Read, you should read through the Focus Questions to get an idea of the concepts you will want to focus on during your second reading. You should work through the Focus Questions by making annotations, highlighting important concepts, and writing notes or questions in the "Notes" column. Depending on instructions from your teacher, you may need to respond online or use a separate piece of paper to start expanding on your thoughts and ideas.

⑥ WRITING PROMPT

Your study of each excerpt or selection will end with a writing assignment. To complete this assignment, you should use your notes, annotations, and answers to both the Think and Focus Questions. Be sure to read the prompt carefully and address each part of it in your writing assignment.

ENGLISH LANGUAGE DEVELOPMENT TEXTS

The English Language Development texts and activities take a closer look at the language choices that authors make to communicate their ideas. Individual and group activities will help develop your understanding of each text.

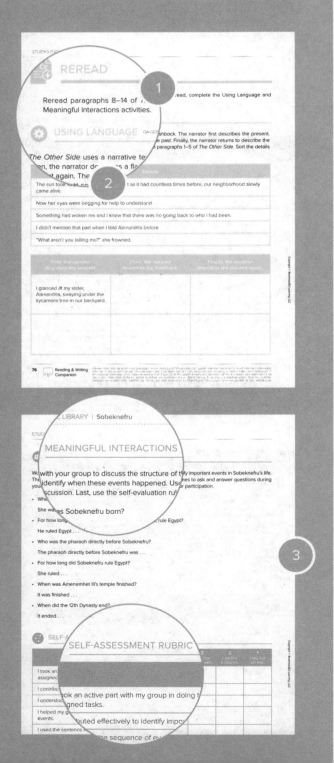

1 REREAD

After you have completed the First Read, you will have two additional opportunities to revisit portions of the excerpt more closely. The directions for each reread will specify which paragraphs or sections you should focus on.

2 USING LANGUAGE

These questions will ask you to analyze the author's use of language and conventions in the text. You may be asked to write in sentence frames, fill in a chart, or you may simply choose between multiple-choice options. To answer these questions, you should read the exercise carefully and go back in the text as necessary to accurately complete the activity.

3 MEANINGFUL INTERACTIONS & SELF-ASSESSMENT RUBRIC

After each reading, you will participate in a group activity or discussion with your peers. You may be provided speaking frames to guide your discussions or writing frames to support your group work. To complete these activities, you should revisit the excerpt for textual evidence and support. When you finish, use the Self-Assessment Rubric to evaluate how well you participated and collaborated.

EXTENDED WRITING PROJECT

The Extended Writing Project is your opportunity to explore the theme of each unit in a longer written work. You will draw information from your readings, research, and own life experiences to complete the assignment.

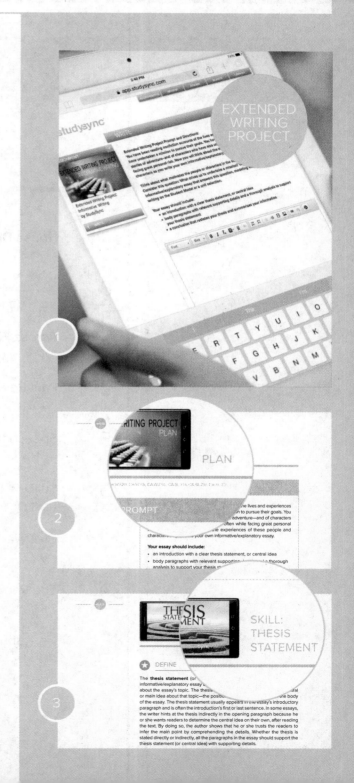

1 WRITING PROJECT

After you have read all of the unit text selections, you will move on to a writing project. Each project will guide you through the process of writing an argumentative, narrative, informative, or literary analysis essay. Student models and graphic organizers will provide guidance and help you organize your thoughts as you plan and write your essay. Throughout the project, you will also study and work on specific writing skills to help you develop different portions of your writing.

2 WRITING PROCESS STEPS

There are five steps in the writing process: **Prewrite**, **Plan**, **Draft**, **Revise**, and **Edit, Proofread, and Publish**. During each step, you will form and shape your writing project so that you can effectively express your ideas. Lessons focus on one step at a time, and you will have the chance to receive feedback from your peers and teacher.

3 WRITING SKILLS

Each Writing Skill lesson focuses on a specific strategy or technique that you will use during your writing project. The lessons begin by analyzing a student model or mentor text, and give you a chance to learn and practice the skill on its own. Then, you will have the opportunity to apply each new skill to improve the writing in your own project.

UNIT 4   How did the War Between the States redefine America?

The Civil War

TEXTS

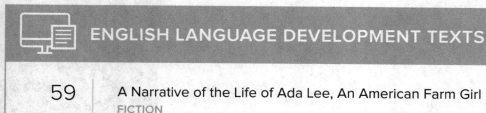

ENGLISH LANGUAGE DEVELOPMENT TEXTS

 EXTENDED WRITING PROJECT

 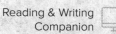

HOUSE DIVIDED SPEECH

INTRODUCTION

Abraham Lincoln delivered his famous speech, "House Divided," in 1858, when tensions were running high before the start of the Civil War. Lincoln explained the use of the "house divided" imagery in this way: "I want to use some universally known figure, expressed in simple language as universally known, that it may strike home to the minds of men in order to rouse them to the peril of the times." This excerpt reproduces the introduction, which contains the best-known passage, and the close of Lincoln's speech.

"A house divided against itself cannot stand."

 ## FIRST READ

1 Mr. President and Gentlemen of the Convention.

2 If we could first know where we are, and **whither** we are tending, we could then better judge what to do, and how to do it.

3 We are now far into the fifth year, since a **policy** was initiated, with the avowed object, and confident promise, of putting an end to slavery **agitation**.

4 Under the operation of that policy, that agitation has not only, not ceased, but has constantly **augmented**.

5 In my opinion, it will not cease, until a crisis shall have been reached, and passed.

6 "A house divided against itself cannot stand."

7 I believe this government cannot endure, permanently half slave and half free.

8 I do not expect the Union to be dissolved—I do not expect the house to fall— but I do expect it will cease to be divided.

9 It will become all one thing or all the other.

10 Either the opponents of slavery, will arrest the further spread of it, and place it where the public mind shall rest in the belief that it is in the course of ultimate extinction; or its **advocates** will push it forward, till it shall become alike lawful in all the States, old as well as new—North as well as South.

11 . . .

Reading & Writing
Companion

NOTES

12 Our cause, then, must be intrusted to, and conducted by its own undoubted friends—those whose hands are free, whose hearts are in the work—who do care for the result.

13 Two years ago the Republicans of the nation mustered over thirteen hundred thousand strong.

14 We did this under the single impulse of resistance to a common danger, with every external circumstance against us.

15 Of strange, discordant, and even, hostile elements, we gathered from the four winds, and formed and fought the battle through, under the constant hot fire of a disciplined, proud, and pampered enemy.

16 Did we brave all then to falter now?—now—when that same enemy is wavering, dissevered and belligerent?

17 The result is not doubtful. We shall not fail—if we stand firm, we shall not fail.

18 Wise councils may accelerate or mistakes delay it, but, sooner or later the victory is sure to come.

THINK QUESTIONS   CA-CCSS: CA.RI.8.1, CA.L.8.4a, CA.L.8.4b

1. To whom is Abraham Lincoln speaking and why is he addressing them? Cite textual evidence to support your answer.

2. According to Lincoln, which issue is dividing or splitting the nation, and why? Cite evidence from the text in your response.

3. What does Lincoln predict will happen to the country if this issue is not rectified, or corrected? Include evidence from the text to support your response.

4. Use the antonym of "opponents" to determine the meaning of the word **advocates** as it is used in the "House Divided" speech. Explain how you figured out the word's meaning and write your definition. List some other synonyms of "advocates."

5. Remembering that the Latin suffix *-tion* means "act" or "process," use the dictionary definition of the term *agitate* to determine the meaning of **agitation**, and write its definition.

CLOSE READ CA-CCSS: CA.RI.8.1, CA.RI.8.4, CA.RI.8.5, CA.RI.8.6, CA.W.8.4, CA.W.8.5, CA.W.8.6, CA.W.8.10

Reread the speech "House Divided." As you reread, complete the Focus Questions below. Then use your answers and annotations from the questions to help you complete the Writing Prompt.

FOCUS QUESTIONS

1. As you reread the text of the "House Divided" speech, remember that Abraham Lincoln uses a particular text structure to present information. Analyze the structure of a few specific paragraphs. What is the effect of the structure on the speech? Highlight evidence in the text to show the structure and make annotations to explain how the structure affects the speech.

2. Formal language can contribute to the tone of a text. Highlight words or phrases from the first part of the excerpt that are examples of formal language. What is the effect of the language on the tone? Make annotations to explain your ideas.

3. Highlight words or phrases from the second excerpt that are examples of formal language. Then make annotations to explain how these word choices contribute to the tone of the text.

4. How does the tone of the speech and the use of allusion help readers understand Lincoln's point of view about slavery? Highlight textual evidence that supports your understanding. Write an annotation to explain how the author uses tone and allusion to convey his meaning.

5. Think about the structure, tone, and content of Lincoln's speech. How might Lincoln's speech of 1858 have helped redefine the United States? Write an annotation to explain your answer. Then highlight evidence from the text that helps support your ideas.

WRITING PROMPT

In the "House Divided" speech, Abraham Lincoln wrote about an issue that he felt strongly about and that was very important to him. Write a short speech about a topic that is important to you, using specific word choice to convey tone. Choose an informational text structure that helps communicate and develop your ideas clearly in each paragraph. In your speech, include an allusion or image that you think conveys the situation in a powerful and memorable way. Make it your goal to persuade your audience to accept your point of view.

Please note that excerpts and passages in the StudySync® library and this workbook are intended as touchstones to generate interest in an author's work. The excerpts and passages do not substitute for the reading of entire texts, and StudySync® strongly recommends that students seek out and purchase the whole literary or informational work in order to experience it as the author intended. Links to online resellers are available in our digital library. In addition, complete works may be ordered through an authorized reseller by filling out and returning to StudySync® the order form enclosed in this workbook.

Reading & Writing Companion   **7**

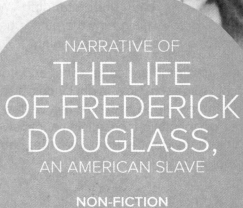

NARRATIVE OF
THE LIFE
OF FREDERICK
DOUGLASS,
AN AMERICAN SLAVE

NON-FICTION
Frederick Douglass
1845

INTRODUCTION

Published in 1845, the autobiography, *Narrative of the Life of Frederick Douglass, an American Slave*, describes Douglass's journey from slavery to freedom. This great American orator provides a factual account of his struggle to educate and free himself and others from the oppression of his times. The memoir's vivid descriptions of life as a slave played a key role in fueling the abolitionist movement in the North prior to the Civil War. In the following excerpt from the middle of the text, Douglass overcomes the odds against him, procuring the assistance of others in teaching himself to read despite laws prohibiting slaves from learning such skills.

"The more I read, the more I was led to abhor and detest my enslavers."

 FIRST READ

 NOTES

1   The plan which I adopted, and the one by which I was most successful, was that of making friends of all the little white boys whom I met in the street. As many of these as I could, I converted into teachers. With their kindly aid, obtained at different times and in different places, I finally succeeded in learning to read. When I was sent of errands, I always took my book with me, and by going one part of my errand quickly, I found time to get a lesson before my return. I used also to carry bread with me, enough of which was always in the house, and to which I was always welcome; for I was much better off in this regard than many of the poor white children in our neighborhood. This bread I used to bestow upon the hungry little urchins, who, in return, would give me that more valuable bread of knowledge. I am strongly tempted to give the names of two or three of those little boys, as a testimonial of the gratitude and affection I bear them; but **prudence** forbids;— not that it would injure me, but it might embarrass them; for it is almost an unpardonable offence to teach slaves to read in this Christian country. It is enough to say of the dear little fellows, that they lived on Philpot Street, very near Durgin and Bailey's ship-yard. I used to talk this matter of slavery over with them. I would sometimes say to them, I wished I could be as free as they would be when they got to be men. "You will be free as soon as you are twenty-one, but I am a slave for life! Have not I as good a right to be free as you have?" These words used to trouble them; they would express for me the liveliest sympathy, and console me with the hope that something would occur by which I might be free.

2   I was now about twelve years old, and the thought of being a slave for life began to bear heavily upon my heart. Just about this time, I got hold of a book entitled "The Columbian **Orator**." Every opportunity I got, I used to read this book. Among much of other interesting matter, I found in it a dialogue between a master and his slave. The slave was represented as having run away from his master three times. The dialogue represented the conversation which took place between them, when the slave was retaken the third time. In this

Please note that excerpts and passages in the StudySync® library and this workbook are intended as touchstones to generate interest in an author's work. The excerpts and passages do not substitute for the reading of entire texts, and StudySync® strongly recommends that students seek out and purchase the whole literary or informational work in order to experience it as the author intended. Links to online resellers are available in our digital library. In addition, complete works may be ordered through an authorized reseller by filling out and returning to StudySync® the order form enclosed in this workbook.

Reading & Writing Companion   9

NOTES

dialogue, the whole argument in behalf of slavery was brought forward by the master, all of which was disposed of by the slave. The slave was made to say some very smart as well as impressive things in reply to his master—things which had the desired though unexpected effect; for the conversation resulted in the voluntary emancipation of the slave on the part of the master.

3   In the same book, I met with one of Sheridan's mighty speeches on and in behalf of Catholic emancipation. These were choice documents to me. I read them over and over again with **unabated** interest. They gave tongue to interesting thoughts of my own soul, which had frequently flashed through my mind, and died away for want of utterance. The moral which I gained from the dialogue was the power of truth over the conscience of even a slaveholder. What I got from Sheridan was a bold **denunciation** of slavery, and a powerful **vindication** of human rights.

4   The reading of these documents enabled me to utter my thoughts, and to meet the arguments brought forward to sustain slavery; but while they relieved me of one difficulty, they brought on another even more painful than the one of which I was relieved. The more I read, the more I was led to abhor and detest my enslavers. I could regard them in no other light than a band of successful robbers, who had left their homes, and gone to Africa, and stolen us from our homes, and in a strange land reduced us to slavery. I loathed them as being the meanest as well as the most wicked of men. As I read and contemplated the subject, behold! that very discontentment which Master Hugh had predicted would follow my learning to read had already come, to torment and sting my soul to unutterable anguish. As I writhed under it, I would at times feel that learning to read had been a curse rather than a blessing. It had given me a view of my wretched condition, without the remedy. It opened my eyes to the horrible pit, but to no ladder upon which to get out. In moments of agony, I envied my fellow-slaves for their stupidity. I have often wished myself a beast. I preferred the condition of the meanest reptile to my own. Any thing, no matter what, to get rid of thinking! It was this everlasting thinking of my condition that tormented me. There was no getting rid of it. It was pressed upon me by every object within sight or hearing, animate or inanimate. The silver trump of freedom had roused my soul to eternal wakefulness. Freedom now appeared, to disappear no more forever. It was heard in every sound, and seen in everything. It was ever present to torment me with a sense of my wretched condition. I saw nothing without seeing it, I heard nothing without hearing it, and felt nothing without feeling it. It looked from every star, it smiled in every calm, breathed in every wind, and moved in every storm.

THINK QUESTIONS CA-CCSS: CA.RI.8.1, CA.RI.8.4, CA.L.8.4, CA.L.8.4b, CA.SL.8.1c, CA.SL.8.1d

1. Identify textual evidence from the excerpt that reveals why learning to read was so important to Frederick Douglass when he was a boy.

2. What parallels, or similarities, do you see between the books Douglass reads and his own life? Cite textual evidence from the excerpt to support the similarities you find.

3. What does Douglass learn about the history of slavery through the books that he reads that lead him to detest his master, even though in some ways, as a boy, Douglass felt he was "much better off" than some of the white boys in his neighborhood. Cite textual evidence to support your answer.

4. Use context to determine the meaning of the word **unabated** as it is used in *Narrative of the Life of Frederick Douglass, An American Slave*. Write your definition of "unabated" and tell how you arrived at it.

5. Remembering that the Latin root *nunci* means "to speak or carry a message" and the prefix *de-* means "from or against," use the context clues provided in the passage to determine the meaning of **denunciation** and write its definition.

CLOSE READ
CA-CCSS: CA.RI.8.1, CA.RI.8.3, CA.RI.8.4, CA.W.8.4, CA.W.8.5, CA.W.8.6, CA.W.8.10

Reread the excerpt from *Narrative of the Life of Frederick Douglass, An American Slave*. As you reread, complete the Focus Questions below. Then use your answers and annotations from the questions to help you complete the Writing Prompt.

FOCUS QUESTIONS

1. Explain the way Douglass infers, through word choice and description, how he regards himself as the equal of the "little white boys" he sees on the street. Highlight textual evidence that supports your answer and write a brief annotation to explain it.

2. Douglass does not begin to detest his slaveholder, and regard his enslavers as the "most wicked of men," until he reads "The Columbian Orator." What is it about this text and its content that really disturbs him, apart from the idea that he might not be able to escape slavery?

3. In the first paragraph, Douglass writes that he does not want to reveal the names of the white boys who taught him to read, because "it is an almost unpardonable offence." What personal comment does Douglass add to this statement? What does he later come to realize when he reads one of Sheridan's speeches in "The Columbian Orator," and what distinctions does he make between these ideas? Highlight textual evidence that supports your answer.

4. Informational texts blend facts and details about events, individuals, and ideas. Each of these details interact and combine in a text, often resulting in cause-and-effect relationships. Trace the cause-and-effect relationships in *Narrative of the Life of Frederick Douglass, An American Slave* and how they result in Douglass feeling tormented "with a sense of my wretched condition." Highlight textual evidence that supports your answer

5. Douglass frequently uses figurative language, and specifically certain figures of speech, to help readers understand his situation in vivid and dramatic ways. Identify the figure of speech Douglass uses in the third paragraph of the excerpt. What does it mean, and in what way does it indicate an important turning point in his life? Highlight textual evidence that supports your answer and write a brief annotation to explain it.

WRITING PROMPT

In some informational texts, authors try to persuade readers to accept a specific point of view about a subject. In what way does Frederick Douglass use elements of figurative language to express the anger and torment that he feels, and help readers understand it? How does the use of these figures of speech strengthen his argument against slavery? Use your understanding of figurative language and informational text elements to determine how successfully Douglass uses them in his narrative. Support your writing with evidence from the text.

ACROSS FIVE APRILS

FICTION
Irene Hunt
1964

INTRODUCTION

With two brothers fighting in the Civil War, one for the North and one for the South, 9-year-old Jethro Creighton finds himself the only son remaining in a house as divided as the country. Following the war through newspaper articles, and weathering the conflicts at home on the family farm in Illinois, Jethro takes his first steps into manhood. In this excerpt, news of the war enters the Creighton's kitchen conversation.

"There is an awakenin' inside us of human decency and responsibility."

NOTES

FIRST READ

From Chapter 2

where were the two brothers at? why were the two brothers separated?

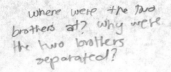

Why were Jenny & Nancy getting the "comp'ny supper" ready? What does the author mean when he said "a couple of chickens had been dressed?"

1 The two older brothers and Wilse Graham talked as they splashed in the cold water, and Jethro could sense the pleasure they felt in seeing one another again after the **lapse** of several years.

2 In the kitchen, Jenny and Nancy hurried about getting the "comp'ny supper" ready. A couple of chickens had been dressed hastily and thrown into the pot; sweet potatoes were set to bake in the hot ashes, and dried apples were cooked in a syrup of wild honey and then topped with thick cream from one of the crocks in the spring house. Nancy made a flat cake of white flour with a sprinkling of sugar on top, and Jenny pulled tender radishes and onions from her garden to give the taste of spring to their meal.

3 A coal-oil lamp was lighted and placed in the middle of the table when supper was at last ready; gold light filled the kitchen, pouring from the open fireplace and from the sparkling lamp chimney. Black shadows hung in the adjoining room where the bed had been spread with Ellen's newest quilt and the pillows dressed in fresh covers in honor of the guest. Jethro was sensitive to color and contrast; the memory of the golden kitchen and the velvet shadows of the room beyond was firmly stamped in his mind.

4 At the table, the talk for a while was of family affairs; there had been a death of someone in Kentucky who was only a name to Jethro, but a name that brought a shadow to his mother's face; there were reports of weddings and births, of tragedies, and now and then a happy note of good fortune. Then the conversation began to turn. Slowly and inevitably the troubles of the nation began to move into the crowded little kitchen.

5 "Will Kaintuck go secesh, Wilse?" Matthew Creighton asked finally, his eyes on his plate.

6   "Maybe, Uncle Matt, maybe it will. And how will southern Illinois feel about it in case that happens?"

7   No one answered. Wilse took a drink of water, and then setting the glass down, twirled it a few times between his thumb and fingers.

8   "It will come hard fer the river states if Missouri and Kaintuck join up with the Confederacy. Ol' Mississippi' won't be the safest place fer north shippin' down to the Gulf."

9   "That's true, Wilse. That's in the minds of a lot of us," Matthew said quietly. Bill's eyes were fixed on the yellow light around the lamp chimney; John was studying his cousin's face.

10   "As fer southern Illinois," Wilse continued, "you folks air closer by a lot to the folks in Missouri and Kaintuck than you are to the bigwigs up in Chicago and northern Illinois. You're southern folks down here."

11   "We're from Kaintuck as you well know, Wilse; our roots air in that state. I'd say that eighty per cent of the folks in this part of the country count Missouri or Kaintuck or Tennessee as somehow bein' their own. But this separation, Wilse, it won't do. We're a union; separate, we're jest two weakened, puny pieces, each needin' the other."

12   "We was a weak and puny country eighty odd years ago when the great-granddaddy of us young uns got mixed up in a rebel's fight. Since then we've growed like weeds in the spring, and what's happened? Well, I'll tell you: a hall of the country has growed rich, favored by Providence, but still jealous and fearful that the other half is apt to find good fortune too. Face it, Uncle Matt; the North has become arrogant toward the South. The high-**tariff** industrialists would sooner hev the South starve than give an inch that might cost them a penny."

13   Then Ellen's voice was heard, timid and a little **tremulous**; farm women didn't enter often into man-talk of politics or national affairs.

14   "But what about the downtrodden people, Wilse? Ain't slavery becomin' more of a festerin' hurt each year? Don't we *hevto* make a move against it?"

15   "Yore own Ol' Abe from this fair state of Illinois is talkin' out of both sides of his mouth—fer the time bein' anyway." Wilse brought his hand down sharply on the table. "What the South wants is the right to live as it sees fit to live without interference. And it kin live! Do you think England won't come breakin' her neck to help the South in case of war? She ain't goin' to see her looms

NOTES

starve fer cotton because the northern industrialists see fit to butt in on a way of life that the South has found good. Believe me, Uncle Matt; the South kin fight fer years if need be—till this boy here is a man growed with boys of his own."

16 Young Tom's face was red with anger, but a warning look from his mother kept him quiet. From the far end of the table, however, John's voice came, strained and a little unnatural.

17 "You hev hedged Ma's question, Cousin Wilse. What about the right and wrong of one man ownin' the body—and sometimes it looks as if the soul, too—of another man?"

18 Wilse hesitated a moment, his eyes on the plate of food, which he had barely touched during the last few minutes. "I'll say this to you, Cousin John," he said finally. "I own a few slaves, and if I stood before my Maker alongside one of em, I'd hev no way to justify the fact that I was master and he was slave. But leavin' that final **reckonin'** fer the time, let me ask you this: ain't there been slavery from the beginnin' of history? Didn't the men that we give honor to, the men that shaped up the Constitution of our country, didn't they recognize slavery? Did they see it as a festerin' hurt?"

19 "Some of em did, I reckon," John answered gravely. "I can't help but believe that some of em must not ha' been comftable with them words 'a peculiar institution.'"

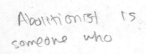

Abolitionist is someone who

20 "Well then, I'll ask you this: if tomorrow every slave in the South had his freedom and come up North, would yore **abolitionists** git the crocodile tears sloshed out of their eyes so they could take the black man by the hand? Would they say, 'We'll see that you git good-payin' work fitted to what you're able to do—we'll see that you're well housed and clothed—we want you to come to our churches and yore children to come to our schools, why, we danged near fergit the difference in the colors of our skins because we air so almighty full of brotherly love!' Would it be like that in yore northern cities, Cousin John?"

21 "It ain't like that fer the masses of white people in our northern cities—nor in the southern cities either. And yet, there ain't a white man, lean-bellied and hopeless as so many of them are, that would change lots with a slave belongin' to the kindest master in the South."

22 Then Bill spoke for the first time, his eyes still on the yellow light of the lamp.

23 "Slavery, I hate. But it is with us, and them that should suffer fer the evil they brought to our shores air long dead. What I want us to answer in this year of 1861 is this, John: does the trouble over slavery come because men's hearts

is purer above the Mason-Dixon line? Or does slavery throw a shadder over greed and keep that greed from showin' up quite so bare and ugly?"

24   Wilse Graham seemed to leap at Bill's question. "You're right, Cousin Bill. It's greed, not slavery, that's stirrin' up this trouble. And as fer human goodness—men's hearts is jest as black today as in the Roman times when they nailed slaves to crosses by the hunderd and left them there to point up a lesson.

Members of the Creighton family are so divided about the idea of secession from the Union.

25   Matt Creighton shook his head. "Human nature ain't any better one side of a political line than on the other—we all know that—but human nature, the all-over picture of it, *is* better than it was a thousand—five hundred—even a hundred years ago. There is an awakenin' inside us of human decency and responsibility. If I didn't believe that, I wouldn't grieve fer the children I've buried; I wouldn't look for'ard to the manhood of this youngest one."

human nature changed throughout the years

people were treated badly thousands of years, but they're treated better throughout the years

*people starts to realize the mistakes they made*

Excerpted from *Across Five Aprils* by Irene Hunt, published by The Berkley Publishing Group.

Think Questions #1-3

THINK QUESTIONS   CA-CCSS: CA.RL.8.1, CA.L.8.4a

1. Why are members of the Creighton family so divided about the idea of secession from the Union? Cite textual evidence to support your answer.

2. Use details from the text to write two or three sentences that describe the differing points of view the members of the Graham family have toward slavery.

3. Write two or three sentences comparing Bill and Matthew's views on the possibility of a war between North and South. Cite textual evidence that reveals their views.

4. Use context clues to determine the meaning of the word **tremulous** as it is used in *Across Five Aprils*. Write your definition of "tremulous" and explain how you arrived at it.

5. Determine the meaning of the word **abolitionist** as it is used in *Across Five Aprils*, using context clues in the text. Write your definition of "abolitionist" and explain how you arrived at it.

CLOSE READ

CA-CCSS: CA.RL.8.1, CA.RL.8.3, CA.RL.8.6, CA.W.8.3, CA.W.8.4, CA.W.8.5, CA.W.8.6, CA.W.8.10

Reread the excerpt from *Across Five Aprils*. As you reread, complete the Focus Questions below. Then use your answers and annotations from the questions to help you complete the Writing Prompt.

FOCUS QUESTIONS

1. The bond between family members is apparent in this excerpt from *Across Five Aprils*. How does using third-person limited omniscient point of view help reveal this bond? Highlight textual evidence to support your ideas and write annotations to explain your choices.

2. Wilse Graham is reluctant to answer Ellen's question about slavery becoming more of a "festerin' hurt" each year, and whether or not "we hev to make a move against it." How does the author reveal that Wilse feels in his heart that slavery is wrong, even though he defends it as an economic necessity? Highlight evidence from the text that will help support your answer.

3. In the sixteenth paragraph, one of Ellen and Matthew's sons has a reaction to what his cousin Wilse says in the previous paragraph. What does this reaction reveal about the family and about how the character of Bill Creighton stands apart from what the rest of what his family believes? Highlight textual evidence to support your ideas, and make annotations to explain your choices.

4. An author creates characters through dialogue and their reactions to plot events. What situation has provoked Wilse and John to argue about slavery? What do their differing attitudes toward slavery reveal about each man's character? Highlight textual evidence to support your ideas and make annotations to explain your choices.

5. In the last paragraph of the excerpt, Matt Creighton makes his final statement on human decency and the evils of slavery. How does the author make use of dramatic irony in this statement, as a way of foreshadowing, or giving readers a hint, of the Civil War to come and of the many ways it will change the country? Highlight textual evidence and make annotations to support your explanation.

WRITING PROMPT

Think about how the various characters in this excerpt from *Across Five Aprils* feel about the institution of slavery and the prospect of civil war. Imagine what might happen if, as war is declared, Jethro Creighton announces to his family that he intends to enlist in the Union army. Establish a context and point of view and organize a sequence of events that unfolds naturally and logically after Jethro's announcement, based on the traits of the characters you have read about. How might Matt feel about Jethro's decision? Use your understanding of point of view and character traits in your narrative, as well as techniques such as dialogue, pacing, description, and reflection to develop experiences, events and the characters in your story.

PAUL REVERE'S RIDE

POETRY
Henry Wadsworth Longfellow
1861

INTRODUCTION

Henry Wadsworth Longfellow is considered the first professional American poet and, thanks to "Paul Revere's Ride", one of the most popular of his time. Just weeks after Longfellow finished the poem, Abraham Lincoln won the presidency. America was on the verge of the Civil War. An abolitionist, Longfellow published the work not only to commemorate the actions of Paul Revere on the eve of the Revolution, but to inspire Americans to fight for the Union and to abolish slavery. The poet took intentional liberties in his telling of the story, greatly enhancing the actual historical events and creating an American hero in the process. Notable for both its poetic form and its link between the two great wars fought on American soil, "Paul Revere's Ride" has inspired generations of readers with its vivid portrayal of an American hero's call to arms.

"One, if by land, and two, if by sea..."

 FIRST READ

NOTES

1 Listen, my children, and you shall hear
2 Of the midnight ride of Paul Revere,
3 On the eighteenth of April, in Seventy-Five;
4 Hardly a man is now alive
5 Who remembers that famous day and year.

6 He said to his friend, "If the British march
7 By land or sea from the town to-night,
8 Hang a lantern aloft in the belfry arch
9 Of the North Church tower, as a signal light, —
10 One, if by land, and two, if by sea;
11 And I on the opposite shore will be,
12 Ready to ride and spread the alarm
13 Through every Middlesex village and farm,
14 For the country-folk to be up and to arm."

15 Then he said "Good-night!" and with muffled oar
16 Silently rowed to the Charlestown shore,
17 Just as the moon rose over the bay,
18 Where swinging wide at her **moorings** lay
19 The Somerset, British man-of-war;
20 A phantom ship, with each mast and spar
21 Across the moon like a prison-bar,   ← simile
22 And a huge black hulk, that was magnified
23 By its own reflection in the tide.

24 Meanwhile, his friend, through alley and street
25 Wanders and watches with eager ears,
26 Till in the silence around him he hears
27 The muster of men at the barrack door,

28 The sound of arms, and the tramp of feet,
29 And the measured tread of the **grenadiers,**
30 Marching down to their boats on the shore.

31 Then he climbed the tower of the Old North Church,
32 By the wooden stairs, with stealthy tread,
33 To the belfry-chamber overhead,
34 And startled the pigeons from their perch
35 On the somber rafters, that round him made
36 Masses and moving shapes of shade, —
37 By the trembling ladder, steep and tall,
38 To the highest window in the wall,
39 Where he paused to listen and look down
40 A moment on the roofs of the town,
41 And the moonlight flowing over all.

42 Beneath, in the churchyard, lay the dead,
43 In their night-encampment on the hill,
44 Wrapped in silence so deep and still
45 That he could hear, like a sentinel's tread,
46 The watchful night-wind, as it went
47 Creeping along from tent to tent,
48 And seeming to whisper, "All is well!"
49 A moment only he feels the spell
50 Of the place and the hour, the secret dread
51 Of the lonely belfry and the dead;
52 For suddenly all his thoughts are bent
53 On a shadowy something far away,
54 Where the river widens to meet the bay, —
55 A line of black, that bends and floats
56 On the rising tide, like a bridge of boats.

57 Meanwhile, impatient to mount and ride,
58 Booted and spurred, with a heavy stride
59 On the opposite shore walked Paul Revere.
60 Now he patted his horse's side,
61 Now gazed on the landscape far and near,
62 Then, **impetuous,** stamped the earth,
63 And turned and tightened his saddle-girth;
64 But mostly he watched with eager search
65 The belfry-tower of the Old North Church,
66 As it rose above the graves on the hill,
67 Lonely and **spectral** and **somber** and still.
68 And lo! as he looks, on the belfry's height
69 A glimmer, and then a gleam of light!

NOTES

70 He springs to the saddle, the bridle he turns,
71 But lingers and gazes, till full on his sight
72 A second lamp in the belfry burns!

73 A hurry of hoofs in a village street,
74 A shape in the moonlight, a bulk in the dark,
75 And beneath, from the pebbles, in passing, a spark
76 Struck out by a steed flying fearless and fleet:
77 That was all! And yet, through the gloom and the light,
78 The fate of a nation was riding that night;
79 And the spark struck out by that steed, in his flight,
80 Kindled the land into flame with its heat.

81 He has left the village and mounted the steep,
82 And beneath him, tranquil and broad and deep,
83 Is the Mystic, meeting the ocean tides;
84 And under the alders that skirt its edge,
85 Now soft on the sand, now loud on the ledge,
86 Is heard the tramp of his steed as he rides.

87 It was twelve by the village clock,
88 When he crossed the bridge into Medford town.
89 He heard the crowing of the cock,
90 And the barking of the farmer's dog,
91 And felt the damp of the river fog,
92 That rises after the sun goes down.

93 It was one by the village clock,
94 When he galloped into Lexington.
95 He saw the gilded weathercock
96 Swim in the moonlight as he passed,
97 And the meeting-house windows, blank and bare,
98 Gaze at him with a spectral glare,
99 As if they already stood aghast
100 At the bloody work they would look upon.

101 It was two by the village clock,
102 When he came to the bridge in Concord town.
103 He heard the bleating of the flock,
104 And the twitter of birds among the trees,
105 And felt the breath of the morning breeze
106 Blowing over the meadow brown.
107 And one was safe and asleep in his bed
108 Who at the bridge would be first to fall,
109 Who that day would be lying dead,
110 Pierced by a British musket-ball.

NOTES

111 You know the rest. In the books you have read,
112 How the British regulars fired and fled, —
113 How the farmers gave them ball for ball,
114 From behind each fence and farm-yard wall,
115 Chasing the red-coats down the lane,
116 Then crossing the fields to emerge again
117 Under the trees at the turn of the road,
118 And only pausing to fire and load.

119 So through the night rode Paul Revere;
120 And so through the night went his cry of alarm
121 To every Middlesex village and farm, —
122 A cry of defiance and not of fear,
123 A voice in the darkness, a knock at the door,
124 And a word that shall echo forevermore!
125 For, borne on the night-wind of the Past,
126 Through all our history, to the last,
127 In the hour of darkness and peril and need,
128 The people will waken and listen to hear
129 The hurrying hoof-beat of that steed,
130 And the midnight-message of Paul Revere.

THINK QUESTIONS CA-CCSS: CA.RL.8.1, CA.L.8.4a, CA.SL.8.1c, CA.SL.8.1d

1. What details does Longfellow include to explain the time and place in which the events of the poem take place? Support your answer with evidence from the text.

2. What does Longfellow mean when he writes that Revere's friend wanders and watches through alley and street "with eager ears"? What does he hear that causes him to climb the tower of the Old North Church? Support your answer with evidence from the text.

3. Use details from the poem to write two or three sentences that describe how Longfellow felt about Paul Revere.

4. Use context to determine the meaning of the word **moorings** as it is used in "Paul Revere's Ride." Write your definition of "moorings" and explain how you figured it out.

5. Determine the meaning of the word **impetuous** as it is used in this poem. Write your definition of "impetuous" and explain how you figured it out.

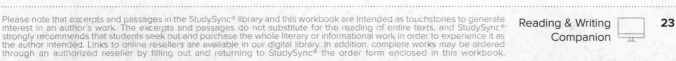
Please note that excerpts and passages in the StudySync® library and this workbook are intended as touchstones to generate interest in an author's work. The excerpts and passages do not substitute for the reading of entire texts, and StudySync® strongly recommends that students seek out and purchase the whole literary or informational work in order to experience it as the author intended. Links to online resellers are available in our digital library. In addition, complete works may be ordered through an authorized reseller by filling out and returning to StudySync® the order form enclosed in this workbook.

Reading & Writing Companion   **23**

CLOSE READ   CA-CCSS: CA.RL.8.1, CA.RL.8.4, CA.L.8.4a, CA.L.8.5b, CA.L.8.5c, CA.W.8.4, CA.W.8.5, CA.W.8.6, CA.W.8.10

Reread the poem "Paul Revere's Ride." As you reread, complete the Focus Questions below. Then use your answers and annotations from the questions to help you complete the Writing Prompt.

 FOCUS QUESTIONS

1. Longfellow uses many figures of speech in "Paul Revere's Ride," including similes and personification. Find an example of a simile in the third stanza and an example of personification in the eleventh stanza. What images do these two examples of figurative language create? How do they add to the meaning of the poem? Cite textual evidence and annotate to support your answer.

2. The denotation, or dictionary definition, of the word pierced is "to make a hole in; to bore into or through." The word pierced can have a positive connotation when referring, for example, to a light that pierced the darkness. Does Longfellow's use of pierced in line 110 of the twelfth stanza have a negative or a positive connotation? What does his word choice add to the poem? Use textual evidence to support your answer.

3. Longfellow substitutes the word steed for horse once Paul Revere begins his famous ride to warn the people of Middlesex and its surrounding villages that the British are coming. How does the substitution of this word affect the meaning and tone of the poem? Annotate your answer and use textual evidence to support it.

4. The word aghast can have multiple denotative meanings: to be stunned or astonished; to be horrified at something; to be amazed; to be startled. What meaning of the word aghast does Longfellow use in line 99 of the eleventh stanza? Does it have a positive or a negative connotation? Use evidence from the text to support your answer.

5. Longfellow uses the word tread twice in the poem. "Tread" has a number of denotative meanings, including "to walk; to crush; to step on or through; to step across something; to trample." Sometimes the relationship between words can help readers understand the word's denotative and connotative meanings. In the fifth stanza, how does the adjective *stealthy* help define the word *tread* in line 32, and what kind of connotative meaning does it give the word the way it is used in the poem? Support your answer with textual evidence.

6. "Paul Revere's Ride" was first published just as the Civil War was beginning. What words or phrases does Longfellow use in the poem to create a dramatic tone that would resonate with a nation on the brink of Civil War? Highlight your answers and annotate to show how his poem was also capturing the drama of a nation full of civil unrest.

WRITING PROMPT

How does Henry Wadsworth Longfellow's use of language in "Paul Revere's Ride" set the tone for the events described in the poem? How does the poet use connotation and denotation to create visual images that add to the meaning of the poem? Use your understanding of figurative language as well as connotation and denotation to determine how the author's word choices impact meaning and tone. Support your writing with evidence from the text.

AIN'T I A WOMAN

NON-FICTION
Sojourner Truth
1851

INTRODUCTION

The first women's rights convention in the United States was held in Seneca Falls, New York, in 1848. Many of the attendees signed a document arguing for equal rights for women, including the right to vote. The document, called the Declaration of Sentiments, summoned people from around the country to organize conventions that would urge lawmakers, clergy, and journalists to support the cause. Three years later, at one such assembly in Akron, Ohio, former slave Sojourner Truth gave a rousing and memorable speech. Two accounts are provided here.

"I can't read, but I can hear."

 FIRST READ

Account by Frances Dana Gage, *Anti-Slavery Standard*, 1863

1   Well, children, where there is so much racket there must be something out of kilter. I think that **'twixt** the negroes of the South and the women at the North, all talking about rights, the white men will be in a fix pretty soon. But what's all this here talking about?

2   That man over there says that women need to be helped into carriages, and lifted over ditches, and to have the best place everywhere. Nobody ever helps me into carriages, or over mud-puddles, or gives me any best place! And ain't I a woman? Look at me! Look at my arm! I have ploughed and planted, and gathered into barns, and no man could head me! And ain't I a woman? I could work as much and eat as much as a man - when I could get it - and bear the lash as well! And ain't I a woman? I have borne thirteen children, and seen most all sold off to slavery, and when I cried out with my mother's grief, none but Jesus heard me! And ain't I a woman?

3   Then they talk about this thing in the head; what's this they call it? [Member of audience whispers, "intellect."] That's it, honey. What's that got to do with women's rights or negroes' rights? If my cup won't hold but a pint, and yours holds a quart, wouldn't you be mean not to let me have my little half measure full?

4   Then that little man in black there, he says women can't have as much rights as men, 'cause Christ wasn't a woman! Where did your Christ come from? Where did your Christ come from? From God and a woman! Man had nothing to do with Him.

5   If the first woman God ever made was strong enough to turn the world upside down all alone, these women together ought to be able to turn it back, and get it right side up again! And now they is asking to do it, the men better let them.

6 **Obliged** to you for hearing me, and now old Sojourner ain't got nothing more to say.

Account by Marius Robinson, *Anti-Slavery Bugle*, 1851:

7 I want to say a few words about this matter. I am for a woman's rights. I have as much muscle as any man, and can do as much work as any man. I have plowed and reaped and husked and chopped and mowed, and can any man do more than that? I have heard much about the sexes being equal. I can carry as much as any man, and can eat as much too, if I can get it. I am as strong as any man that is now.

8 As for intellect, all I can say is, if a woman have a pint, and a man a quart—why can't she have her little pint full? You need not be afraid to give us our rights for fear we will take too much—for we can't take more than our pint'll hold.

9 The poor men seems to be all in confusion and don't know what to do. Why children, if you have woman's rights, give it to her and you will feel better. You will have your own rights, and they won't be so much trouble.

10 I can't read, but I can hear. I have heard the Bible and have learned that Eve caused man to sin. Well, if woman upset the world, do give her a chance to set it right side up again. The lady has spoken about Jesus, how he never **spurned** woman from him, and she was right. When Lazarus died, Mary and Martha came to him with faith and love and **besought** him to raise their brother. And Jesus wept and Lazarus came forth. And how came Jesus into the world? Through God who created him and the woman who bore him. Man, where was your part?

11 But the women are coming up, blessed be God, and a few of the men are coming up with them. But man is in a tight place, the poor slave is on him, woman is coming on him, he is surely between a hawk and a **buzzard.**

THINK QUESTIONS CA-CCSS: CA.RI.8.1, CA.L.8.4a, CA.L.8.5b, CA.SL.8.1a, CA.SL.8.1b, CA.SL.8.1c, CA.SL.8.1d

1. Use details from the text to summarize Sojourner Truth's opinion about men thinking "women need to be helped into carriages, and lifted over ditches, and to have the best place everywhere."

2. Why are there two versions of the speech?

3. Refer to two or more details in the text to support the idea that, in some ways, Sojourner Truth thinks women are actually stronger than men.

4. Use context to determine the meaning of the word **obliged** as it is used in Sojourner Truth's speech to the Ohio Women's Conference. Write your definition of "obliged" and explain how you arrived at it.

5. Use context clues to determine the meaning of the word **intellect** as it is used in the third paragraph of Truth's speech. Write your definition of "intellect" and explain how you arrived at it.

CLOSE READ   CA-CCSS: CA.RI.8.1, CA.RI.8.9, CA.W.8.4, CA.W.8.5, CA.W.8.6, CA.W.8.10

Reread the two accounts of Truth's speech. As you reread, complete the Focus Questions below. Then use your answers and annotations from the questions to help you complete the Writing Prompt.

FOCUS QUESTIONS

1. Do you think the repetition of the words "Ain't I a Woman?" make the first account more effective to the reader or audience member than the second account? Cite textual evidence from both versions of Sojourner Truth's speech to support your answer.

2. How did Truth's faith help her make an argument for women's rights? What is the difference between both accounts of the speech? Use textual evidence from both accounts to support your answer.

3. Annotate each paragraph of the first account of Truth's speech to explain how each one supports her message about women's rights.

4. According to the text, what makes Sojourner Truth feel that she is equal to a man? Cite textual evidence from both accounts to support your answer, and explain how they differ.

5. Explain the following sentence from the second account: "As for intellect, all I can say is, if a woman have a pint and a man a quart—why can't she have her little pint full?" Highlight the text in the first account that expresses the same information.

6. How does the first paragraph of Gage's account foreshadow the changes that are coming, with the Civil War just around the corner? Highlight evidence and annotate to support your answer.

WRITING PROMPT

Consider Sojourner Truth's statement in the first account: "If my cup won't hold but a pint, and yours holds a quart, wouldn't you be mean not to let me have my little half measure full?" What does she mean by "cup, pint, and quart?" How does Robinson present this idea in the second account, and how is the meaning of Sojourner Truth's statement changed slightly in Robinson's account? Write an explanation of the analogies that Truth makes and compare and contrast the two accounts of the speech and how they present these analogies. Then write an answer to the second question, comparing the two presentations. Use textual evidence to support your answer.

SULLIVAN BALLOU LETTER

NON-FICTION
Sullivan Ballou
1861

INTRODUCTION

Rhode Islander Sullivan Ballou was an officer in the Union Army during the Civil War. He is best remembered for an eloquent letter he wrote to his wife in July, 1861, in which Ballou describes the conflicting pulls of duty to country and love of his wife. A week after he wrote the letter, Ballou was killed at the first

"Not my will, but thine, O God be done."

NOTES

FIRST READ

July 14, 1861

Camp Clark, Washington

1 My very dear Sarah:

2 The indications are very strong that we shall move in a few days—perhaps tomorrow. Lest I should not be able to write again, I feel **impelled** to write a few lines that may fall under your eye when I am no more. Our movements may be of a few days' duration and full of pleasure—and it may be of some conflict and death to me. "Not my will, but thine, O God be done." If it is necessary that I should fall on the battlefield for my Country, I am ready.

3 I have no **misgivings** about, or lack of confidence in the cause in which I am engaged, and my courage does not halt or falter. I know how strongly American Civilization now leans on the triumph of the Government and how great a debt we owe to those who went before us through the blood and suffering of the Revolution. And I am willing—perfectly willing—to lay down all my joys in this life, to help maintain this government, and to pay that debt.

4 Sarah my love for you is deathless, it seems to bind me with mighty cables that nothing but **Omnipotence** could break; and yet my love of Country comes over me like a strong wind and bears me unresistibly on with all these chains to the battlefield.

5 The memories of the blissful moments I have spent with you come creeping over me, and I feel most gratified to God and to you that I have enjoyed them for so long. And hard it is for me to give them up and burn to ashes the hopes of future years, when, God willing, we might still have lived and loved together, and seen our sons grown up to honorable manhood, around us. I have, I know, but few and small claims upon Divine Providence, but something

NOTES

whispers to me—perhaps it is the **wafted** prayer of my little Edgar, that I shall return to my loved ones unharmed. If I do not my dear Sarah, never forget how much I love you, and when my last breath escapes me on the battlefield, it will whisper your name. Forgive my many faults and the many pains I have caused you. How thoughtless and foolish I have often times been! How gladly would I wash out with my tears every little spot upon your happiness and struggle with all the misfortunes of this world to shield you and your children from harm. But I cannot. I must watch you from the Spirit-land and hover near you, while you buffet the storm, with your precious little freight, and wait with sad patience till we meet to part no more.

6   But, O Sarah! If the dead can come back to this earth and **flit** unseen around those they loved, I shall always be near you; in the gladdest days and in the darkest nights. . . always, always, and if there be a soft breeze upon your cheek, it shall be my breath, as the cool air fans your throbbing temple, it shall be my spirit passing by. Sarah do not mourn me dead; think I am gone and wait for thee, for we shall meet again.

7   As for my little boys—they will grow up as I have done, and never know a father's love and care. Little Willie is too young to remember me long, and my blue-eyed Edgar will keep my frolics with him among the deep memories of childhood. Sarah, I have unlimited confidence in your maternal care and your development of their character, and feel that God will bless you in your holy work.

8   Tell my two Mothers I call God's blessing upon them. O! Sarah. I wait for you there; come to me and lead thither my children.

9   Sullivan

 THINK QUESTIONS   CA-CCSS: CA.RI.8.1, CA.RI.8.4, CA.L.8.5a

1. What is the purpose behind Sullivan Ballou's letter to his wife? Cite textual evidence to support your answer.

2. Cite textual evidence that explains why Ballou tells his wife that she should not mourn him when he is dead.

3. Is Sullivan Ballou proud of his life and his family? Cite textual evidence to support your answer.

4. In Paragraph 3, Ballou uses the word **Omnipotence** to refer to God. That is why it is capitalized even though it appears in the middle of a sentence. **Omnipotence** comes from a Latin word that means "all" and from the Latin root poten-, which means "powerful" and "capable." The same root is found in the words *potency* and *potential*. Write your definition of "Omnipotence" and explain how you arrived at it.

5. Use context in the selection to determine the meaning of the word **flit** as it is used in "Sullivan Ballou Letter." Write your definition and explain how you arrived at it, citing textual evidence.

Please note that excerpts and passages in the StudySync® library and this workbook are intended as touchstones to generate interest in an author's work. The excerpts and passages do not substitute for the reading of entire texts, and StudySync® strongly recommends that students seek out and purchase the whole literary or informational work in order to experience it as the author intended. Links to online resellers are available in our digital library. In addition, complete works may be ordered through an authorized reseller by filling out and returning to StudySync® the order form enclosed in this workbook.

Reading & Writing Companion   31

CLOSE READ   CA-CCSS: CA.RI.8.1, CA.RI.8.2, CA.RI.8.3, CA.RI.8.4, CA.RI.8.7, CA.L.8.2a, CA.L.8.2b, CA.W.8.4, CA.W.8.5, CA.W.8.6, CA.W.8.10

Reread the letter from Sullivan Ballou. As you reread, complete the Focus Questions below. Then use your answers and annotations from the questions to help you complete the Writing Prompt.

FOCUS QUESTIONS

1. Explain how Sullivan Ballou uses the first two paragraphs in his letter to indicate that he understands the seriousness of his situation, and yet is determined to follow through on the task he has set for himself. How does Sullivan provide a transition to the third paragraph where he changes the subject to his feelings for his wife Sarah? Highlight textual evidence to support your answer.

2. What kind of punctuation does Sullivan use to highlight and emphasize the depth of his feelings? Why would this kind of punctuation not appear very often in a tweet or text message, and how would its absence affect the emotion and feelings expressed in Sullivan's letter?

3. Although Sullivan wrote this letter to comfort his wife, in what way does the letter also reveal what the risks were, and why the war was so important for many fighting on the Union side? Why do you think it was important for Sullivan to mention these things to his wife? Use textual evidence to support your answer.

4. Sullivan's sons Edgar and Willie are important subjects in this letter, even though it is not addressed to them. Why are they important? Why might Sullivan leave out this information if this were a text message to his wife? Highlight textual evidence to support your answers.

5. Sullivan uses many kinds of figurative language in his letter. For example, he fears the hopes he has for many more years with his wife may be "burned to ashes," as if they were something physical that could actually be burned. What kind of analogy does Sullivan use in the sixth paragraph? Highlight textual evidence and make annotations to explain your ideas.

What does Ballou mean when he says that "American Civilization now leans on the triumph of the Government?" Why does he link the Civil War to the American Revolution as "a debt to America that must be repaid"?

WRITING PROMPT

On the basis of the letter that Ballou wrote to his wife, do you think he feels that he led a good, fulfilling life? As you explain, use evidence from the text to support your response.

CIVIL WAR JOURNAL

NON-FICTION
Louisa May Alcott
1861–1863

INTRODUCTION

Louisa May Alcott is best known for her semi-autobiographical novel *Little Women*, but she also authored numerous other works and kept extensive journals about her life. Like many women who wanted to participate during the Civil War, Alcott volunteered as a nurse and served six weeks at a Union hospital in Washington, D.C. These excerpts from her personal journals document some of her experiences during the tumultuous period in American history.

"I've often longed to see a war, and now I have my wish."

FIRST READ

1   *April.* [1861]—War declared with the South, and our Concord **company** went to Washington. A busy time getting them ready, and a sad day seeing them off, for in a little town like this we all seem like one family in times like these. At the station the scene was very dramatic, as the brave boys went away perhaps never to come back again.

2   I've often longed to see a war, and now I have my wish. I long to be a man, but as I can't fight, I will content myself with working for those who can. . . .

3   *September, October.* [1862]—. . . War news bad. Anxious faces, beating heart, and busy minds.

4   I like the stir in the air, and long for battle like a warhorse when he smells powder. The blood of the Mays is up!

5   *November.*—Thirty years old. Decided to go to Washington as a nurse if I could find a place. Help needed, and I love nursing, and *must* let out my pent-up energy in some new way. Winter is always a hard and a dull time, and if I am away there is one less to feed and warm and worry over.

6   I want new experiences, and am sure to get 'em if I go. So I've sent in my name, and bide my time writing tales, to leave all snug behind me, and mending up my old clothes,—for nurses don't need nice things, thank Heaven!

7   *December.*—On the 11th I received a note from Miss H. M. Stevenson telling me to start for Georgetown next day to fill a place in the Union Hotel Hospital. Mrs. Ropes of Boston was matron, and Miss Kendall of Plymouth was a nurse there, and though a hard place, help was needed. I was ready, and when my commander said "March!" I marched. Packed my trunk, and reported in B.[oston] that same evening.

8   We had all been full of courage till the last moment came, then we all broke down. I realized that I had taken my life in my hand, and might never see them all again. I said, "Shall I stay, Mother?" as I hugged her close. "No, go! And the Lord be with you!" answered the **Spartan** woman, and till I turned the corner she bravely smiled and waved her wet handkerchief on the doorstep. Shall I ever see that dear old face again?

9   So I set forth in the December twilight, with May and Julian Hawthorne as an escort, feeling as if I was the son of the house going to war.

10   Friday, the 12th, was a very memorable day, spent in running all over Boston to get my pass, etc., calling for parcels, getting a tooth filled, and buying a veil,—my only purchase. A.C. gave me some old clothes, the dear Sewalls money for myself and boys, lots of love and help, and at 5 P.M., saying "goodby" to a group of tearful faces at the station, I started on my long journey, full of hope and sorrow, courage and plans.

11   A most interesting journey into a new world full of stirring sights and sounds, new adventures, and an ever growing sense of the great task I had undertaken.

12   I said my prayers as I went rushing through the country white with tents, all alive with patriotism, and already red with blood.

13   A solemn time, but I'm glad to live in it, and am sure it will do me good whether I come out alive or dead.

14   All went well, and I got to Georgetown one evening very tired. Was kindly welcomed, slept in my narrow bed with two other room-mates, and on the morrow began my new life by seeing a poor man die at dawn, and sitting all day between a boy with pneumonia and a man shot through the lungs. A strange day, but I did my best, and when I put mother's little black shawl round the boy while he sat up panting for breath, he smiled and said, "You are real motherly, ma'am." I felt as if I was getting on. The man only lay and stared with his big black eyes, and made me very nervous. But all were well behaved, and I sat looking at the twenty strong faces as they looked back at me,— hoping that I looked "motherly" to them, for my thirty years made me feel old, and the suffering round me made me long to comfort every one. . . .

15   *January.* [1863]—I never began the year in a stranger place than this, five hundred miles from home, alone among strangers, doing painful duties all day long, & leading a life of constant excitement in this greathouse surrounded by 3 or 4 hundred men in all stages of suffering, disease & death. Though often home sick, heart sick & worn out, I like it—find real pleasure in comforting tending & cheering these poor souls who seem to love me, to feel my sympathy though unspoken, & acknowledge my hearty good will in spite of the ignorance, awkwardness, & bashfulness which I cannot help showing in

so new & trying a situation. The men are docile, respectful, & affectionate, with but few exceptions, truly lovable & manly many of them. John Suhre a Virginia blacksmith is the prince of patients, & though what we call a common man, in education & condition, to me is all that I could expect or ask from the first gentleman in the land. Under his plain speech & unpolished manner I seem to see a noble character, a heart as warm & tender as a woman's, a nature fresh & frank as any child's. He is about thirty, I think, tall & handsome, mortally wounded & dying royally, without **reproach**, repining, or remorse. Mrs. Ropes & myself love him & feel indignant that such a man should be so early lost, for though he might never distinguish himself before the world, his influence and example cannot be without effect, for real goodness is never wasted.

16   Mon 4th—I shall record the events of a day as a sample of the days I spend— Up at six, dress by gas light, run through my ward & fling up the windows though the men grumble & shiver; but the air is bad enough to breed a **pestilence** & as no notice is taken of our frequent appeals for better ventilation I must do what I can. Poke up the fire, add blankets, joke, coax, & command, but continue to open doors & windows as if life depended on it; mine does, & doubtless many another, for a more perfect pestilence-box than this house I never saw—cold, damp, dirty, full of vile odors from wounds, kitchens, wash rooms, & stables. No competent head, male or female, to right matters, & a jumble of good, bad, & indifferent nurses, surgeons & attendants to complicate the Chaos still more.

17   After this unwelcome progress through my **stifling** ward I go to breakfast with what appetite I may; find the inevitable fried beef, salt butter, husky bread & washy coffee; listen to the clack of eight women & a dozen men; the first silly, stupid or possessed of but one idea, the last absorbed in their breakfast & themselves to a degree that is both ludicrous and provoking, for all the dishes are ordered down the table *full* & returned *empty*; the conversation is entirely among themselves & each announces his opinion with an air of importance that frequently causes me to choke up in my cup or bolt my meals with undignified speed lest a laugh betray to these pompous beings that a "child's among them takin notes." Till noon I trot, trot, giving out rations, cutting up food for helpless "boys," washing faces, teaching my attendants how beds are made or floor swept, dressing wounds, taking Dr. Fitz Patrick's orders, (privately wishing all the time that he would be more gentle with my big babies,) dusting tables, sewing bandages, keeping my tray tidy, rushing up & down after pillows, bed linen, sponges, books & directions, till it seems as if I would joyfully pay down all I possess for fifteen minutes rest.

18   At twelve the big bell rings & up comes dinner for the boys who are always ready for it & never entirely satisfied. Soup, meat, potatoes, & bread is the bill of fare. Charley Thayer the attendant travels up & down the room serving out

NOTES

the rations, saving little for himself yet always thoughtful of his mates & patient as a woman with their helplessness. When dinner is over some sleep, many read, & others want letters written. This I like to do for they put in such odd things & express their ideas so comically I have great fun interiorly while as grave as possible exteriorly. A few of the men word their paragraphs well & make excellent letters. John's was the best of all I wrote. The answering of letters from friends after some one has died is the saddest & hardest duty a nurse has to do.

19 Supper at five sets every one to running that can run & when that flurry is over all settle down for the evening amusements which consist of newspapers, gossip, Drs last round, & for such as need them the final doses for the night. At nine the bell rings, gas is turned down & day nurses go to bed.

20 Night nurses go on duty, & sleep & death have the house all to themselves. . . .

21 My work is changed to night watching or half night & half day, from twelve to twelve. I like it as it leaves me time for a morning run which is what I need to keep well, for bad air, food, water, work & watching are getting to be too much for me. I trot up & down the streets in all directions, some times to the Heights, then half way to Washington, again to the hill over which the long trains of army wagons are constantly vanishing & ambulances appearing.

22 That way the fighting lies, & long to follow. . . .

THINK QUESTIONS   CA-CCSS: CA.RI.8.1, CA.RI.8.4, CA.L.8.5

1. Refer to one or more details in the text to support your understanding of why Louisa May Alcott was anxious to participate, in some way, in the Civil War—both from ideas that are explicitly stated and from ideas that you have inferred from clues in the text.

2. In paragraphs 7–10, Alcott bids an emotional goodbye to her mother and then journeys to Boston to prepare for her trip. Why is leaving such a big decision for Louisa? What does her decision say about her character? Cite textual evidence to support your answer.

3. As Louisa May Alcott begins her duties in Georgetown, she feels conflicting emotions. Cite evidence from the text that shows how she feels at the beginning of the new year, 1863.

4. Use context to determine the meaning of the word **Spartan** as it is used in "Civil War Journal." Write your definition of **Spartan** and tell how you arrived at it.

5. Alcott describes the ward she works in as a **pestilence**-box. Use context clues in the text to determine the meaning of **pestilence**, and explain how you found it.

CLOSE READ
CA-CCSS: CA.RI.8.1, CA.RI.8.3, CA.RI.8.4, CA.RI.8.5, CA.RI.8.6, CA.W.8.4, CA.W.8.5, CA.W.8.6, CA.W.8.10

Reread the excerpt from *Civil War Journal*. As you reread, complete the Focus Questions below. Then use your answers and annotations from the questions to help you complete the Writing Prompt.

FOCUS QUESTIONS

1. A journal is a daily record. If it is not kept for business reasons, it is often private and, like a diary, records the writer's personal feelings and reactions to events. Journals often feature informal language and may even contain run-on sentences and other grammatical errors. Find features of journal writing in Louisa May Alcott's "Civil War Journal" that give it an informal tone, and support your answers with textual evidence.

2. What does Alcott reveal in her January 4th entry about the difficulty of her days in the ward, and also the fact that she may want to take her journal entries and turn them into a book one day? Support your answer with textual evidence.

3. Highlight and annotate Alcott's descriptions of the soldiers she treats. How does she make distinctions between each of these individuals?

4. What does Louisa May Alcott's attitude toward her duties in the ward, as well as the last sentence in this excerpt, reveal about her character? Highlight textual evidence to support your answer.

5. Write an annotation to explain how the last sentence of the journal contributes to Alcott's overall text structure.

6. The Civil War changed the way many Americans felt about war and about themselves. At the beginning of her journal, what were Alcott's feelings about war and about her role in the war? How did the war and her time as a nurse for Union soldiers encourage Alcott to redefine herself? Highlight textual evidence to support your answer.

WRITING PROMPT

Consider the events that take place in Alcott's *Civil War Journal*. How do these events and the way they are presented help to indicate the text structure she employs in her writing? Give specific examples to support your answer.

THE RED BADGE OF COURAGE

FICTION

Stephen Crane

1895

INTRODUCTION

Published in 1894, the Civil War novel *The Red Badge of Courage* was popularized through a serial release in hundreds of newspapers throughout the country. Although author Stephen Crane never witnessed a battle, his vivid descriptions of war and the psychology of its soldiers captured readers' imaginations and brought home the stark realities of America's bloody divide. The story follows young Private Henry Fleming as he experiences firsthand the horrors of battle and a personal crisis of will. In these excerpts we join Henry on his journey through both internal and external landscapes in pursuit of courage.

"So he went far, seeking dark and intricate places."

 FIRST READ

Excerpt from Chapter 1

1   There was a youthful private who listened with eager ears to the words of the tall soldier and to the varied comments of his comrades. After receiving a fill of discussions concerning marches and attacks, he went to his hut and crawled through an intricate hole that served it as a door. He wished to be alone with some new thoughts that had lately come to him.

2   He lay down on a wide bunk that stretched across the end of the room. In the other end, cracker boxes were made to serve as furniture. They were grouped about the fireplace. A picture from an illustrated weekly was upon the log walls, and three rifles were paralleled on pegs. Equipments hung on handy projections, and some tin dishes lay upon a small pile of firewood. A folded tent was serving as a roof. The sunlight, without, beating upon it, made it glow a light yellow shade. A small window shot an oblique square of whiter light upon the cluttered floor. The smoke from the fire at times neglected the clay chimney and wreathed into the room, and this flimsy chimney of clay and sticks made endless threats to set ablaze the whole establishment.

3   The youth was in a little trance of astonishment. So they were at last going to fight. On the morrow, perhaps, there would be a battle, and he would be in it. For a time he was obliged to labor to make himself believe. He could not accept with assurance an omen that he was about to mingle in one of those great affairs of the earth.

4   He had, of course, dreamed of battles all his life—of vague and bloody conflicts that had thrilled him with their sweep and fire. In visions he had seen himself in many struggles. He had imagined peoples secure in the shadow of his eagle-eyed prowess. But awake he had regarded battles as crimson blotches on the pages of the past. He had put them as things of the bygone with his thought-images of heavy crowns and high castles. There was a portion of the

world's history which he had regarded as the time of wars, but it, he thought, had been long gone over the horizon and had disappeared forever.

5   From his home his youthful eyes had looked upon the war in his own country with distrust. It must be some sort of a play affair. He had long despaired of witnessing a Greeklike struggle. Such would be no more, he had said. Men were better, or more timid. Secular and religious education had effaced the throat-grappling instinct, or else firm finance held in check the passions.

6   He had burned several times to enlist. Tales of great movements shook the land. They might not be distinctly Homeric, but there seemed to be much glory in them. He had read of marches, sieges, conflicts, and he had longed to see it all. His busy mind had drawn for him large pictures extravagant in color, **lurid** with breathless deeds.

7   But his mother had discouraged him. She had affected to look with some contempt upon the quality of his war **ardor** and patriotism. She could calmly seat herself and with no apparent difficulty give him many hundreds of reasons why he was of vastly more importance on the farm than on the field of battle. She had had certain ways of expression that told him that her statements on the subject came from a deep conviction. Moreover, on her side, was his belief that her ethical motive in the argument was **impregnable**.

8   At last, however, he had made firm rebellion against this yellow light thrown upon the color of his ambitions. The newspapers, the gossip of the village, his own picturings, had aroused him to an uncheckable degree. They were in truth fighting finely down there. Almost every day the newspaper printed accounts of a decisive victory.

Excerpt from Chapter 7

9   The youth cringed as if discovered in a crime. By heavens, they had won after all! The imbecile line had remained and become victors. He could hear cheering.

10 He lifted himself upon his toes and looked in the direction of the fight. A yellow fog lay wallowing on the treetops. From beneath it came the clatter of musketry. Hoarse cries told of an advance.

11 He turned away amazed and angry. He felt that he had been wronged.

12 He had fled, he told himself, because annihilation approached. He had done a good part in saving himself, who was a little piece of the army. He had considered the time, he said, to be one in which it was the duty of every little piece to rescue itself if possible. Later the officers could fit the little pieces together again, and make a battle front. If none of the little pieces were wise

Please note that excerpts and passages in the StudySync® library and this workbook are intended as touchstones to generate interest in an author's work. The excerpts and passages do not substitute for the reading of entire texts, and StudySync® strongly recommends that students seek out and purchase the whole literary or informational work in order to experience it as the author intended. Links to online resellers are available in our digital library. In addition, complete works may be ordered through an authorized reseller by filling out and returning to StudySync® the order form enclosed in this workbook.

Reading & Writing
Companion

41

enough to save themselves from the flurry of death at such a time, why, then, where would be the army? It was all plain that he had proceeded according to very correct and commendable rules. His actions had been **sagacious** things. They had been full of strategy. They were the work of a master's legs.

13 Thoughts of his comrades came to him. The brittle blue line had withstood the blows and won. He grew bitter over it. It seemed that the blind ignorance and stupidity of those little pieces had betrayed him. He had been overturned and crushed by their lack of sense in holding the position, when intelligent deliberation would have convinced them that it was impossible. He, the enlightened man who looks afar in the dark, had fled because of his superior perceptions and knowledge. He felt a great anger against his comrades. He knew it could be proved that they had been fools.

14 He wondered what they would remark when later he appeared in camp. His mind heard howls of derision. Their density would not enable them to understand his sharper point of view.

15 He began to pity himself acutely. He was ill used. He was trodden beneath the feet of an iron injustice. He had proceeded with wisdom and from the most righteous motives under heaven's blue only to be frustrated by hateful circumstances.

16 A dull, animal-like rebellion against his fellows, war in the abstract, and fate grew within him. He shambled along with bowed head, his brain in a tumult of agony and despair. When he looked loweringly up, quivering at each sound, his eyes had the expression of those of a criminal who thinks his guilt little and his punishment great, and knows that he can find no words.

17 He went from the fields into a thick woods, as if resolved to bury himself. He wished to get out of hearing of the crackling shots which were to him like voices.

18 The ground was cluttered with vines and bushes, and the trees grew close and spread out like bouquets. He was obliged to force his way with much noise. The creepers, catching against his legs, cried out harshly as their sprays were torn from the barks of trees. The swishing saplings tried to make known his presence to the world. He could not **conciliate** the forest. As he made his way, it was always calling out protestations. When he separated embraces of trees and vines the disturbed foliages waved their arms and turned their face leaves toward him. He dreaded lest these noisy motions and cries should bring men to look at him. So he went far, seeking dark and intricate places.

19 After a time the sound of musketry grew faint and the cannon boomed in the distance. The sun, suddenly apparent, blazed among the trees. The insects

were making rhythmical noises. They seemed to be grinding their teeth in unison. A woodpecker stuck his impudent head around the side of a tree. A bird flew on lighthearted wing.

20   Off was the rumble of death. It seemed now that Nature had no ears.

THINK QUESTIONS   CA-CCSS: CA.RL.8.1, CA.L.8.4a, CA.L.8.4b, CA.SL.8.1a, CA.SL.8.1c, CA.SL.8.1d, CA.SL.8.3

1. Refer to one or more details in Chapter 1 that describe the narrator's ideas about war, both before he joins the army and when he finds out he'll actually be going into battle. Cite textual evidence that is directly stated as well as inferences you have made from clues in the text.

2. At first, the narrator looks on the Civil War with distrust, as if it were some "play affair." What happens to change his mind about the war and encourage him to enlist? Cite textual evidence to support your answer.

3. Why does Henry consider his fellow soldiers "imbeciles," or "the imbecile line" after they manage to win the battle in which Henry was also fighting? Support your answer with textual evidence.

4. Use context clues to determine the meaning of the word **ardor** as it is used in *The Red Badge of Courage*. Write your definition of **ardor** and tell how you arrived at it.

5. Remembering that the Latin prefix *im-* means "not," use the context clues provided in the passage to determine the meaning of **impregnable.** Write your definition of impregnable and explain how you arrived at it.

CLOSE READ
CA-CCSS: CA.RL.8.1, CA.RL.8.2, CA.RL.8.3, CA.RL.8.4, CA.W.8.4, CA.W.8.5, CA.W.8.6, CA.W.8.10, CA.L.8.2c, CA.L.8.5a

Reread the excerpt from *The Red Badge of Courage*. As you reread, complete the Focus Questions below. Then use your answers and annotations from the questions to help you complete the Writing Prompt.

FOCUS QUESTIONS

1. As you reread Chapter 7 of *The Red Badge of Courage*, highlight the following sentences in paragraphs 9 and 11: *The youth cringed as if discovered in a crime. He turned away amazed and angry. He felt that he had been wronged.* How do these three sentences reveal how conflicted Henry feels after he runs away from the battle? In what way do they provide clues about the central theme? Cite textual evidence to support your answer.

2. In paragraph 12, Henry feels that his actions had been full of strategy. He thinks "they were the work of a master's legs." What does he mean by this figure of speech? How is Henry attempting to convince himself that his actions were praise-worthy? Support your answer with textual evidence.

3. What do Henry's conclusions about how the other soldiers will react when he returns to camp reveal about his character? Highlight textual evidence to explain your answer.

4. How does the author use personification to highlight the inner conflict Henry feels as he runs farther and farther away from the battle, and into the woods? Highlight textual evidence and make annotations to explain your answer.

5. What is the overarching theme of this excerpt from *The Red Badge of Courage*? Highlight specific evidence from the text to support your answer. Then make annotations to state the theme in one or two sentences.

6. The Civil War challenged and changed many Americans. How do the soldier's conflicts about war reflect the conflicts of many Americans during this time period? Highlight specific evidence from the text to support your answer.

WRITING PROMPT

How does the point of view Stephen Crane uses in *The Red Badge of Courage* help you understand the thoughts, reactions, and feelings of Private Henry Fleming? How does the use of personification contribute to the text? Use your understanding of point of view and personification to determine the themes that emerge in this excerpt. Support your writing with evidence from the text.

GETTYSBURG ADDRESS

NON-FICTION

Abraham Lincoln
1863

INTRODUCTION

On November 19, 1863, Abraham Lincoln gives perhaps the most famous speech in American history. Evoking the spirit of the nation's founding fathers, Lincoln stands beside the quiet Civil War battlefield of Gettysburg, Pennsylvania and consecrates the hallowed ground to the sacrifice of the soldiers who fought and died there. Reasserting the commitment to preserve the Union and the pursuit of the principles for which it was founded, the elegant words of the Gettysburg Address stand as testament to the greatest challenge in American history.

"[G]overnment of the people, by the people, for the people, shall not perish from the earth."

 FIRST READ

1 Four **score** and seven years ago our fathers brought forth on this continent, a new nation, conceived in liberty, and dedicated to the **proposition** that all men are created equal.

2 Now we are engaged in a great civil war, testing whether that nation, or any nation so conceived and so dedicated, can long endure. We are met on a great battlefield of that war. We have come to dedicate a portion of that field, as a final resting place for those who here gave their lives that that nation might live. It is altogether fitting and proper that we should do this.

3 But in a larger sense, we cannot dedicate - we cannot **consecrate**- we cannot **hallow**- this ground. The brave men, living and dead, who struggled here, have consecrated it, far above our poor power to add or detract. The world will little note, nor long remember what we say here, but it can never forget what they did here. It is for us, the living, rather to be dedicated here to the unfinished work which they who fought here have thus far so nobly advanced.

4 It is rather for us to be here dedicated to the great task remaining before us, that from these honored dead we take increased **devotion** to that cause for which they gave the last full measure of devotion; that we here highly resolve that these dead shall not have died in vain; that this nation, under God, shall have a new birth of freedom, and that government of the people, by the people, for the people, shall not perish from the earth.

THINK QUESTIONS   CA-CCSS: CA.RI.8.1, CA.RI.8.4, CA.L.8.4a, CA.L.8.5b, CA.SL.8.1d, CA.SL.8.2, CA.SL.8.3

1. Write two or three sentences explaining why Lincoln was giving the Gettysburg address. Cite textual evidence to support your answer.

2. Using textual evidence, describe what Lincoln felt the nation should do to prevent the fallen soldiers from having "died in vain."

3. Lincoln said that "in a larger sense," he and the others gathered at Gettysburg "cannot" do something. What was it that they could not do, and why not, according to Lincoln? What did he say they should do instead? Cite textual evidence to support your answer.

4. Use the context of the use of the word **proposition** in the first sentence to determine its definition. Write its definition and indicate the context clues that helped you arrive at this meaning.

5. Based on the relationships among the words *dedicate, consecrate*, and *hallow* in the context of the third paragraph, what might be some synonyms for **consecrate?** How does using synonyms help you understand the word and check for meaning?

Please note that excerpts and passages in the StudySync® library and this workbook are intended as touchstones to generate interest in an author's work. The excerpts and passages do not substitute for the reading of entire texts, and StudySync® strongly recommends that students seek out and purchase the whole literary or informational work in order to experience it as the author intended. Links to online resellers are available in our digital library. In addition, complete works may be ordered through an authorized reseller by filling out and returning to StudySync® the order form enclosed in this workbook.

Reading & Writing Companion   **47**

CLOSE READ

CA-CCSS: CA.RI.8.1, CA.RI.8.2, CA.RI.8.8, CA.W.8.4, CA.W.8.5, CA.W.8.6, CA.W.8.9b, CA.W.8.10, CA.SL.8.3

Reread the text of the Gettysburg Address. As you reread, complete the Focus Questions below. Then use your answers and annotations from the questions to help you complete the Writing Prompt.

FOCUS QUESTIONS

1. As you reread the text of the Gettysburg Address, remember that one of the main ideas is that the Civil War is being fought to preserve the Union. What are some aspects of the text that seem to fit this main idea? Highlight evidence to support your ideas and write annotations to explain your choices.

2. Highlight some key details in paragraph 3 of the text. Then use your details to write a one- or two-sentence summary of that paragraph.

3. Identify a different main idea than the one discussed in Question #1. Annotate each paragraph of the text to explain how each one supports this main idea.

4. Lincoln argues that the war must continue. Highlight evidence that he uses to support this argument. Annotate each piece of evidence to explain how it proves this claim.

5. How does Lincoln believe that the Civil War will redefine America? Highlight Lincoln's claim about how the nation will change after the war. In your annotation, summarize his argument in your own words.

WRITING PROMPT

Choose one paragraph of the Gettysburg Address. What is the main idea of the paragraph? How does this main idea tie to a larger argument Lincoln is making throughout the entire speech? Focus specifically on the structure of the paragraph and how the sentences in the paragraph build on each other to convey the main idea. Respond in an argumentative essay of 300 words. Support your ideas with evidence from the text.

CHASING LINCOLN'S KILLER

NON-FICTION
James L. Swanson
2009

INTRODUCTION

James L. Swanson's fascination with the assassination of Abraham Lincoln traces back to his childhood and the birthday he shares with the famous president. In researching his book, the author pored through trial transcripts, interviews, photographs, and other archival materials to fully understand the circumstances surrounding the infamous events at Ford's Theatre. Here, he takes

"Now, by God, I'll put him through."

FIRST READ

From the Prologue

1 John Wilkes Booth was drinking with a friend at a saloon on Houston Street in New York City. Booth struck the bar table with his fist and regretted a lost opportunity. "What an excellent chance I had, if I wished, to kill the President on Inauguration day! I was on the stand, as close to him nearly as I am to you."

2 Crushed by the fall of Richmond, the former rebel capital, John Wilkes Booth left New York City on April 8 and returned to Washington. The news there was terrible for him. On April 9, Confederate General Robert E. Lee and the Army of Northern Virginia surrendered to Union General Grant at Appomattox. Booth wandered the streets in despair.

3 On April 10, Abraham Lincoln appeared at a second-floor window of the executive mansion, as the White House was known then, to greet a crowd of citizens celebrating General Lee's surrender. Lincoln did not have a prepared speech. He used humor to entertain the audience.

4 On the night of April 11, a torchlight parade of a few thousand people, with bands and banners, assembled on the semi-circular driveway in front of the Executive Mansion. This time Lincoln delivered a long speech, without gloating over the Union victory. He intended to prepare the people for the long task of rebuilding the South. When someone in the crowd shouted that he couldn't see the president Lincoln's son, Tad, volunteered to illuminate his father. When Lincoln dropped each page of his speech to the floor it was Tad who scooped them up.

5 Lincoln described recent events and gave credit to Union General Grant and his officers for the successful end to the war. He also discussed his desire that black people, especially those who had served in the Union army, be granted the right to vote. As Lincoln spoke, one observer, Mrs. Lincoln's

Copyright © BookheadEd Learning, LLC

NOTES

dressmaker, standing a few steps from the president, remarked that the lamplight made him "stand out boldly in the darkness." The perfect target. "What an easy matter would it be to kill the President as he stands there! He could be shot down from the crowd," she whispered," and no one would be able to tell who fired the shot."

6   In that crowd standing below Lincoln was John Wilkes Booth. He turned to his companion, David Herold, and objected to the idea that blacks and former slaves would become voting citizens. In the darkness Booth threatened to kill Lincoln: "Now, by God, I'll put him through."

7   And as Booth left the White House grounds he spoke to companion and co-conspirator, Lewis Powell: "that is the last speech he will ever give."

8   On the evening of April 13, Washington celebrated the end of the war with a grand illumination of the city. Public buildings and private homes glowed from candles, torches, gaslights, and fireworks. It was the most beautiful night in the history of the capital.

9   John Wilkes Booth saw all of this-the grand illumination, the crowds delirious with joy, the insults to the fallen Confederacy and her leaders. He returned to his room at the National Hotel after midnight. He could not sleep.

From Chapter I

10   John Wilkes Booth awoke depressed. It was Good Friday morning, April 14, 1865. The Confederacy was dead. His cause was lost and his dreams of glory over. He did not know that this day, after enduring more than a week of bad news, he would enjoy a stunning reversal of fortune. No, all he knew this morning when he crawled out of bed was that he could not stand another day of Union victory celebrations.

11   Booth assumed that the day would unfold as the latest in a blur of days that had begun on April 3 when the Confederate capital, Richmond, fell to the Union. The very next day, the **tyrant** Abraham Lincoln had visited his captive prize and had the nerve to sit behind the desk occupied by the first and last president of the Confederate States of America, Jefferson Davis. Then, on April 9, at Appomattox Court House, Virginia, General Robert E. Lee and his beloved Army of Northern Virginia surrendered. Two days later, Lincoln had made a speech proposing to give blacks the right to vote and last night, April 13, all of Washington had celebrated with a grand illumination of the city. These days had been the worst in Booth's young life.

12   Twenty-six years old, impossibly vain, an extremely talented actor, and a star member of a celebrated theatrical family, John Wilkes Booth was willing to throw away fame, wealth, and a promising future for the cause of the

Confederacy. He was the son of the legendary actor Junius Brutus Booth and brother to Edwin Booth, one of the finest actors of his generation. Handsome and appealing, he was instantly recognizable to thousands of fans in both the North and South. His physical beauty astonished all who saw him. A fellow actor described his eyes as being "like living jewels." Booth's passions included fine clothing, Southern honor, good manners, beautiful women, and the romance of lost causes.

13 On April 14, Booth's day began in the dining room of the National Hotel, where he ate breakfast. Around noon, he walked over to nearby Ford's Theatre, a block from Pennsylvania Avenue, to pick up his mail: Ford's **customarily** accepted personal mail as a **courtesy** to actors. There was a letter for Booth.

14 That same morning a letter arrived at the theater for someone else. There had been no time to mail it, so its sender, First Lady Mary Todd Lincoln, had used the president's messenger to hand-deliver it to the owners of Ford's Theater. The mere arrival of the White House messenger told them the president was coming to the theater tonight! Yes, the president and Mrs. Lincoln would attend this evening's performance of the popular if silly comedy *Our American Cousin*. But the big news was that General Ulysses S. Grant was coming with them.

15 The Lincolns had given the Fords enough advance notice for the **proprietors** to decorate and join together the two theater boxes — seven and eight — that, by removal of a partition, formed the president's box at the theater.

16 By the time Booth arrived at the Theater, the president's messenger had come and gone. Some time between noon and 12:30 P.M., as he sat on the top step in front of the entrance to Ford's reading his letter, Booth heard the big news: In just eight hours, the man who was the subject of all his hating and plotting would stand on the very stone steps where he now sat. Here. Of all places, Lincoln was coming here.

17 Booth knew the layout of Ford's **intimately**: the exact spot on Tenth Street where Lincoln would step out of his carriage, the box inside the theater where the president sat when he came to a performance, the route Lincoln could walk and the staircase he would climb to the box, the dark underground passageway beneath the stage. He knew the narrow hallway behind the stage where a back door opened to the alley and he knew how the president's box hung directly above the stage.

18 Though Booth had never acted in *Our American Cousin*, he knew it well — its length, its scenes, its players and, most important, the number of actors onstage at any given moment during the performance. It was perfect. He would not have to hunt Lincoln. The president was coming to him.

Excerpted from *Chasing Lincoln's Killer* by James Swanson, published by Scholastic Inc.

 THINK QUESTIONS CA-CCSS: CA.RI.8.1, CA.L.8.4a, CA.L.8.4b

1. What were some of the key events that outraged John Wilkes Booth and led him to decide to assassinate President Lincoln? Cite evidence from the text to support your answer.

2. Why did Booth go to Ford's Theater on the morning of April 14, 1865? What unexpected news did he hear while at the theater? Cite evidence from the text to support your answers.

3. Citing evidence from the text, explain why Ford's Theater was an ideal place for Booth to attempt to assassinate Lincoln.

4. Use context clues in the passage to determine the meaning of the word **tyrant** as it is used in *Chasing Lincoln's Killer*. Write your definition of "tyrant" and explain how you arrived at the definition.

5. Remembering that the Latin suffix *-or* means "a person who has," and also the meaning of the base word *property*, determine the meaning of **proprietor**. Write your definition of "proprietor" and explain how you arrived at it.

Please note that excerpts and passages in the StudySync® library and this workbook are intended as touchstones to generate interest in an author's work. The excerpts and passages do not substitute for the reading of entire texts, and StudySync® strongly recommends that students seek out and purchase the whole literary or informational work in order to experience it as the author intended. Links to online resellers are available in our digital library. In addition, complete works may be ordered through an authorized reseller by filling out and returning to StudySync® the order form enclosed in this workbook.

Reading & Writing Companion 53

CLOSE READ

CA-CCSS: CA.RI.8.1, CA.RI.8.3, CA.RI.8.4, CA.W.8.4, CA.W.8.5, CA.W.8.6, CA.W.8.9b, CA.W.8.10

Reread the excerpt from *Chasing Lincoln's Killer.* As you reread, complete the Focus Questions below. Then use your answers and annotations from the questions to help you complete the Writing Prompt.

FOCUS QUESTIONS

1. Explain how, throughout the text, the author presents the South's defeat in the Civil War as a deeply personal event for John Wilkes Booth. Highlight evidence from the text and make annotations to support your answer.

2. How did John Wilkes Booth's profession help him with his plan to kill the president? Highlight your textual evidence and make annotations to explain your choices.

3. What idea expressed by Lincoln in his speech at the Executive Mansion on the evening of April 11th angered Booth the most? Why did this particular idea anger Booth? Highlight textual

evidence that supports your answer and write an annotation to explain it.

4. What event occurred on April 4th that outraged Booth and, according to the author, made him think of Lincoln as a *tyrant*? Why might Lincoln's action on this day have affected Booth so negatively? Highlight evidence from the text and make annotations to explain your choices.

5. What evidence does the author, James Swanson, include in the passage in support of the idea that John Wilkes Booth was a somewhat reckless person? Highlight details that support your answer and write an annotation to explain it.

WRITING PROMPT

In this excerpt of *Chasing Lincoln's Killer*, how does the author's focus on John Wilkes Booth affect the way the events are developed? Why do you think the author takes this approach? In your analysis, include evidence that is explicitly stated, as well as inferences you draw from the text. Include textual evidence to support your inferences.

O CAPTAIN! MY CAPTAIN!

POETRY
Walt Whitman
1865

INTRODUCTION

studysync tv

Walt Whitman is considered the grandfather of modern American poetry. Largely self-taught, he broke from the traditional strictures of verse, writing long, robust lines brimming with populism, physicality, and personal content. Written to elegize the recently assassinated Abraham Lincoln, "O Captain! My Captain!" strikes a distinctly patriotic note, and marked a departure from Whitman's typical style with its conventional meter and rhyme. The poem was collected into *Leaves of Grass*, of which Whitman wrote, "This is no book; who touches this touches a man."

"O Captain! my Captain! rise up and hear the bells"

 FIRST READ

1 O Captain! my Captain! our fearful trip is done,
2 The ship has **weather'd** every rack, the prize we sought is won,
3 The port is near, the bells I hear, the people all **exulting**,
4 While follow eyes the steady keel, the vessel grim and daring;
5   But O heart! heart! heart!
6   O the bleeding drops of red,
7   Where on the deck my Captain lies,
8   Fallen cold and dead.

9 O Captain! my Captain! rise up and hear the bells;
10 Rise up - for you the flag is flung - for you the bugle **trills**,
11 For you bouquets and ribbon'd wreaths - for you the shores a - crowding,
12 For you they call, the swaying mass, their eager faces turning;
13   Here Captain! dear father!
14   This arm beneath your head!
15   It is some dream that on the deck,
16   You've fallen cold and dead.

17 My Captain does not answer, his lips are pale and still,
18 My father does not feel my arm, he has no pulse nor will,
19 The ship is anchor'd safe and sound, its voyage closed and done,
20 From fearful trip the **victor** ship comes in with object won;
21   Exult O shores, and ring O bells!
22   But I with **mournful** tread,
23   Walk the deck my Captain lies,
24   Fallen cold and dead.

THINK QUESTIONS CA-CCSS: CA.RL.8.1, CA.L.8.4a, CA.SL.8.1a, CA.SL.8.1b, CA.SL.8.1c, CA.SL.8.1d

1. What clues does Walt Whitman provide in the opening stanza of the poem that suggest the captain did not die a natural death? Use textual evidence to support your answer.

2. Describe the details Whitman provides in the second stanza that indicate the fallen Captain was a hero. Use textual evidence to support your answer.

3. In what way does the narrator feel different from the crowds that line the shore waiting for the ship to arrive? Cite details from the text to explain your answer.

4. Use context to determine the meaning of the word **trills** as it is used in "O Captain! My Captain!" Write your definition of "trills" and explain how you arrived at it.

5. Use context to determine the meaning of the word **exulting** as it is used in "O Captain! My Captain!" Write your definition of "exulting" and explain how you arrived at it. Then explain what the port represents in the poem.

CLOSE READ

CA-CCSS: CA.RL.8.1, CA.RL.8.4, CA.RL.8.5, CA.L.8.5c, CA.W.8.4, CA.W.8.5, CA.W.8.6, CA.W.8.10

Reread the poem "Oh Captain! My Captain!" As you reread, complete the Focus Questions below. Then use your answers and annotations from the questions to help you complete the Writing Prompt.

FOCUS QUESTIONS

1. Reread the four indented lines at the end of each stanza in "O Captain! My Captain!". How does each of these show a progression, from the fact of Lincoln's death, the initial disbelief, to the final reluctant acceptance that the "Captain," or president, is dead? What are some of the words, phrases, and poetic devices that Whitman uses to show this progression? Use the annotation tool to paraphrase your responses.

2. Highlight evidence that Walt Whitman uses the metaphor of a captain steering a ship through rough and dangerous weather to explore the idea of a commander-in-chief guiding a nation through a war. Make annotations to explain why this is or is not an effective metaphor.

3. Reread "O Captain! My Captain!", paying close attention to the way Whitman has structured each stanza. Highlight where the structure changes in the poem, and how Whitman shifts between celebration and loss. What effect does this have on the reader? Make annotations to describe how the focus shifts.

4. Reread the first stanza of "O Captain! My Captain!" and highlight the words *exulting* and *vessel*. Use a dictionary to find the denotation of each word. Ask yourself how *exulting* and *vessel* fit into the larger meaning of the poem. What do these words connote in this context? Make annotations to record your reasoning.

5. How does Whitman's use of an apostrophe in the last four lines of the poem connect with his references to both bells and shores earlier in the poem? How do these final four lines in the last stanza fully reveal the narrator's feelings about the poem's events, and indirectly the effects of the Civil War on the country? Use textual evidence to support your answer.

WRITING PROMPT

Walt Whitman uses an extended metaphor in "O Captain! My Captain!" to compare a ship and its captain to a nation and its head of state. Use your understanding of extended metaphor to write a short narrative about an event or a person that you feel deserves a tribute, and how you might use an extended metaphor to write it. Then write one or two stanzas of a poem using this metaphor. Decide on a poetic structure that suits your topic, and use your understanding of connotation and denotation to highlight and emphasize the meaning of the poem.

NARRATIVE OF THE LIFE OF ADA LEE, AN AMERICAN FARM GIRL

English Language
Development

FICTION

INTRODUCTION

The title of "Narrative of the Life of Ada Lee, an American Farm Girl" hints at the autobiography *Narrative of the Life of Frederick Douglass*, an American Slave. This work of historical fiction makes connections between Douglass's efforts to educate himself despite laws that forbade slaves from doing so and Ada's own struggle to pursue a career despite legal and cultural

"I wished that women could do anything we wanted to, and I set out to find a way to change the law..."

 FIRST READ

1   I lowered myself down onto the stool and dug my heels into the barn's dirt floor. "You know I love you, Bessie," I whispered dreamily to our prized dairy cow, "but I'm not going to be with you for much longer. I am going to college." A secret grin spread slowly across my face. It was the first time I had said my plan out loud. "I know what you're thinking, Bessie," I continued, patting her gently. Women could not go to college, but I had heard about a college on the east coast that would accept female students. Even though the school was far away and the workload might be too hard for me given my limited education, I was determined to **enroll**. After all, I had taught myself to read. Learning from a teacher couldn't be harder than that. "It's going to be hard, Bessie, but I will go to college and become a lawyer."

2   Life on the east coast was different than I had expected it to be. I missed my life on the farm terribly, and the pile of law books that rested on my desk practically reached the ceiling. They were filled with **incomprehensible** legal **terminology** that I hadn't much use for when I was back home. I knew I needed to get some help if I were going to succeed. There was a young man in the law program with me who came from a long line of lawyers. His name was John Wilson. I flashed him a wide smile and cleverly told him I'd exchange home-cooked meals for some tutoring. He gladly accepted.

3   John and I worked together intensely from then on. By the time we had earned our law degrees, we had grown quite close. We were married the day after graduation. It was my **earnest** desire that we would open a law office together and continue working side by side. The state legislature, however, had other plans. Even though I had earned a law degree, the state stubbornly would not grant me a license to actually practice law because I was a woman.

4   My husband was not bothered by this turn of events. He had loved studying with me, but he was happy to provide for his family while I ran our home. I was devastated. I didn't have to go to college to be a homemaker. I spent my days bored, **grieving** for the career I'd never have. I wished that I had never heard of the college, because then I'd be a happy wife. But then I wished something else. I wished that women could do anything we wanted to, and I set out to find a way to change the law so we could.

 ## USING LANGUAGE   CA-CCSS: ELD.PI.8.1.Ex

Complete the sentences by filling in the blanks.

1. **Find the sentence in paragraph 1 that tells what Ada did with her plan.**

   It was the first time I _____ my plan out loud.

2. **Find the sentence in paragraph 1 that tells about women's ability to go to college.**

   Women _____ to college, but I had heard about a college on the east coast that _____ female students.

3. **Find the sentence in paragraph 1 that tells why Ada might struggle in college.**

   Even though the school _____ far away and the workload _____ too hard for me given my limited education, I was determined to enroll.

4. **Find the sentence in paragraph 1 that tells how Ada learned to read.**

   After all, I _____ myself _____.

5. **Find the sentence in paragraph 1 that tells what Ada will do.**

   "It's going to be hard, Bessie, but I _____ to college and _____ a lawyer."

Please note that excerpts and passages in the StudySync® library and this workbook are intended as touchstones to generate interest in an author's work. The excerpts and passages do not substitute for the reading of entire texts, and StudySync® strongly recommends that students seek out and purchase the whole literary or informational work in order to experience it as the author intended. Links to online resellers are available in our digital library. In addition, complete works may be ordered through an authorized reseller by filling out and returning to StudySync® the order form enclosed in this workbook.

Reading & Writing Companion   **61**

MEANINGFUL INTERACTIONS   CA-CCSS: ELD.PI.8.1.Ex

Work with your group to discuss your first impressions of the text. First, summarize the major events of the story. Then, discuss what you think of Ada and her struggle. Use the speaking frames to ask and answer relevant questions during your discussion. Last, use the self-assessment rubric to evaluate your participation in the discussion.

- What happens at the beginning of the story?
  At the beginning of the story, Ada . . .

- Where does Ada go?
  Ada goes to . . .

- Who does Ada meet in college? What happens between them?
  Ada meets . . . They . . .

- Why does Ada . . . ?

- What do you think about . . . ?

- I think you said . . . Why do you think that . . . ?

- I agree/disagree because . . .

SELF-ASSESSMENT RUBRIC   CA-CCSS: ELD.PI.8.1.Ex

	4 I did this well.	3 I did this pretty well.	2 I did this a little bit.	1 I did not do this.
I took an active part with others in doing the assigned task.				
I contributed effectively to the group's discussion.				
I asked relevant questions that helped the group understand the story.				
I asked group members relevant questions about what they thought of the story.				
I answered questions clearly.				

REREAD

Reread paragraphs 1 and 2 of "Narrative of the Life of Ada Lee, an American Farm Girl." After you reread, complete the Using Language and Meaningful Interactions activities.

USING LANGUAGE   CA-CCSS: ELD.PII.8.2.a.Ex

Read each quotation from the text and note the referring word in bold. Then complete the chart by choosing the type of referring word from the options and determining the noun that the bolded word refers to.

Type of Referring Word Options	
pronoun	synonym

Quotation	Type of Referring Word	Noun
"I know what you're thinking, Bessie," I continued, patting **her** gently.		
Women could not go to college, but I had heard about a college on the east coast that would accept female students. Even though the **school** was far away and the workload might be too hard for me given my limited education, I was determined to enroll.		
There was a young man in the law program with me **who** came from a long line of lawyers.		
His name was John Wilson. I flashed **him** a wide smile and cleverly told **him** I'd exchange home-cooked meals for some tutoring.		

MEANINGFUL INTERACTIONS CA-CCSS: ELD.PI.8.1.Ex, ELD.PII.8.1.Ex

Work with your group to paraphrase the key ideas and events of the text. Use the speaking frames to guide your discussion. Then complete the structure chart by filling in the major events of the story. Some events have been filled in for you. Last, use the self-assessment rubric to evaluate your participation in the discussion.

- What other words could you use to say . . . ?

- What other words or phrases mean the same as . . . ?

- When did . . . happen?

- Did . . . happen before or after . . . ?

First	Then	Last
Ada sits in the barn.		Ada worries college might be hard.

SELF-ASSESSMENT RUBRIC CA-CCSS: ELD.PI.8.1.Ex

	4 I did this well.	3 I did this pretty well.	2 I did this a little bit.	1 I did not do this.
I took an active part with others in doing the assigned task.				
I contributed effectively to the group's decisions.				
I was able to put events in the right order.				
I paraphrased the key ideas from the text concisely and accurately.				

REREAD

Reread paragraphs 3 and 4 of "Narrative of the Life of Ada Lee, an American Farm Girl." After you reread, complete the Using Language and Meaningful Interactions activities.

USING LANGUAGE   CA-CCSS: ELD.PII.8.2.b.Ex

Read each sentence about the text. Choose the connecting word or phrase that best completes the sentence.

1. _____ Ada and John worked hard, they earned their degrees.

   ○ Because
   ○ While

2. Ada and John graduated _____ they got married.

   ○ before
   ○ therefore

3. Ada hoped they would open a law office _____ continue working together.

   ○ or
   ○ and

4. _____ Ada earned a degree, the state would not give her a license to practice law.

   ○ Even though
   ○ Until

5. John was not bothered, _____ Ada was disappointed.

   ○ since
   ○ but

6. Ada was upset; _____ she set out to change the law.

   ○ likewise
   ○ as a result

Please note that excerpts and passages in the StudySync® library and this workbook are intended as touchstones to generate interest in an author's work. The excerpts and passages do not substitute for the reading of entire texts, and StudySync® strongly recommends that students seek out and purchase the whole literary or informational work in order to experience it as the author intended. Links to online resellers are available in our digital library. In addition, complete works may be ordered through an authorized reseller by filling out and returning to StudySync® the order form enclosed in this workbook.

Reading & Writing Companion   **65**

MEANINGFUL INTERACTIONS CA-CCSS: ELD.PI.8.10.b.Ex, ELD.PII.8.2.b.Ex

Work with a small group to prepare and practice presenting a summary of "Narrative of the Life of Ada Lee, an American Farm Girl." Use the connecting words chart and writing frames that follow to plan your summary. Then, on a separate piece of paper, write your final summary. Write at least three sentences and use at least one connecting word or phrase.

Relationship	Examples
time	as, before, since, finally, meanwhile, when, while, until
sequence	after, first, later, last, next, second, then, third
conclusion	so, in conclusion
contrast	although, but, despite, however, even though, on the other hand
compare	in other words, likewise, similarly
cause	because, due to, for, in order to, since
effect	as a result, if, so, therefore, thus
additional information	also, and, furthermore, in addition
an example	for example, for instance

- First, Ada _____
  _____.

- Ada felt this way because _____
  _____.

- After Ada went to college, _____
  _____.

- Even though Ada worked hard, _____
  _____.

- John felt _____.
  On the other hand, Ada felt _____.

- Finally, _____
  _____.

CATHERINE'S CALLING

English Language
Development

FICTION

INTRODUCTION

How can we stay brave in the face of danger? That is the question faced by a kind young woman who decides to be a nurse during the Civil War. "Catherine's Calling" tells the story of her struggle to persevere as she

"She imagined herself fighting bravely to preserve the Union."

FIRST READ

1 A young woman listened with **eager** ears to the words of President Abraham Lincoln. "The world will little note, nor long remember what we say here, but it can never forget what they did here. It is for us, the living, rather to be dedicated here to the unfinished work which they who fought here have thus far so nobly advanced." Catherine looked at the families gathered in the **graveyard** at Gettysburg to hear the president's address. Death touched each of them. The war had affected every American family. She **yearned** to give them comfort, but she did not know how. She needed to be alone with her thoughts.

2 Catherine closed herself into the small bedroom she shared with her younger sisters. She thought of the men who had given their lives in the battle. Surely if she were a man, she would have joined the army. She imagined herself fighting bravely to preserve the Union. **Patriotism** burned in her chest. She longed to seek honor and glory alongside her countrymen. Her daydream was interrupted when her little sister Sara noisily burst into the room. Sara had fallen and scraped her knee. Catherine carefully wrapped a bandage around the wound. Sara offered a sweet smile. Catherine's heart filled with pride. She realized she did have a way to serve her country. She could volunteer to be a nurse.

3 Safe at home, Catherine had heard cannons in the distance. But she had never heard musket fire that sounded as close as her own heartbeat. Now that she had begun work at the field hospital, gunfire thundered around her. The **barrage** was interrupted only by screams. Catherine tried to stay focused. Her first patient lay before her. The war didn't care that she was scared. It raged on. This man needed help. Catherine reached for a bandage. Suddenly, a bullet tore through the hospital tent. Catherine's feet took flight. It wasn't until she had tucked herself under a nearby weeping willow tree that she realized she had run. She had fled when the soldiers needed her most.

4   Catherine tried to tell herself that it was a **noble** act. If she were killed, there would be one less nurse to tend to the soldiers' wounds. She would return when the **siege** was over. But then she realized something else. She was alone under the tree. None of the other nurses had fled. What would they think of her when she returned? Would they pity her? Would they ever trust her again? Maybe it would be better if she just walked away. Maybe she did not have what it takes to serve after all. Catherine sunk to her knees and wept in the tree's warm embrace.

 USING LANGUAGE   CA-CCSS: ELD.PI.8.6.c.Ex

Read each excerpt from "Catherine's Calling" and note the bold word or phrase. Then use context to choose the correct meaning.

1.   Catherine looked at the families gathered in the graveyard at Gettysburg to hear the president's address. Death **touched each of them**.

   ○ had lost family in the war
   ○ would be killed

2.   She imagined herself fighting bravely to preserve the Union. Patriotism **burned** in her chest.

   ○ felt a strong feeling
   ○ felt pain from a wound

3.   Safe at home, Catherine had heard cannons in the distance. But she had never heard musket fire that **sounded** as close as her own heartbeat

   ○ made the same noise as
   ○ made a noise

4.   Catherine's feet **took flight**. It wasn't until she had tucked herself under a nearby weeping willow tree that she realized she had run.

   ○ flew away
   ○ started to move very quickly

5.   Catherine **sunk** to her knees and wept in the tree's warm embrace.

   ○ went underwater
   ○ lowered down

Please note that excerpts and passages in the StudySync® library and this workbook are intended as touchstones to generate interest in an author's work. The excerpts and passages do not substitute for the reading of entire texts, and StudySync® strongly recommends that students seek out and purchase the whole literary or informational work in order to experience it as the author intended. Links to online resellers are available in our digital library. In addition, complete works may be ordered through an authorized reseller by filling out and returning to StudySync® the order form enclosed in this workbook.

Reading & Writing Companion   **69**

MEANINGFUL INTERACTIONS   CA-CCSS: ELD.PI.8.1.Ex

What does Catherine think war will be like? How well does Catherine's experience as a nurse match up to her expectations? Work in small groups to discuss these questions, using the speaking frames below. Listen carefully to your peers' ideas and respond thoughtfully. Then, use the self-assessment rubric to evaluate your participation in the discussion.

- Before she goes to the war, Catherine imagines . . .

- At the field hospital, Catherine sees . . . and hears . . .

- How does that compare to what Catherine expected . . . ?

- The war is similar to/different than what Catherine expected because . . .

- What did you mean when you said . . . ?

- I agree/disagree because . . .

- You said that . . . I want to add that . . .

SELF-ASSESSMENT RUBRIC   CA-CCSS: ELD.PI.8.1.Ex

	4 I did this well.	3 I did this pretty well.	2 I did this a little bit.	1 I did not do this.
I took an active part with others in doing the activity.				
I contributed effectively to the group's decisions.				
I listened carefully to my peers' ideas.				
I asked appropriate and helpful questions.				
I built on my peers' responses to contribute my own ideas.				

REREAD

Reread paragraphs 1 and 2 of "Catherine's Calling." After you reread, complete the Using Language and Meaningful Interactions activities.

USING LANGUAGE   CA-CCSS: ELD.PII.8.5.Ex

Complete the sentences by filling in the blanks.

1. **Find the sentence in paragraph 1 that tells where Catherine and the families are.**

   Catherine looked at the families gathered _____
   to hear the president's address.

2. **Find the sentence in paragraph 2 that tells how the men lost their lives.**

   She thought of the men who had given their lives _____.

3. **Find the sentence in paragraph 2 that tells how Catherine imagines herself.**

   She imagined herself fighting _____ to preserve the Union.

4. **Find the sentence in paragraph 2 that tells how Sara appeared.**

   Her daydream was interrupted when her little sister Sara _____ burst _____.

5. **Find the sentence in paragraph 2 that tells how Catherine wrapped the bandage.**

   Catherine _____ wrapped a bandage _____.

Please note that excerpts and passages in the StudySync® library and this workbook are intended as touchstones to generate interest in an author's work. The excerpts and passages do not substitute for the reading of entire texts, and StudySync® strongly recommends that students seek out and purchase the whole literary or informational work in order to experience it as the author intended. Links to online resellers are available in our digital library. In addition, complete works may be ordered through an authorized reseller by filling out and returning to StudySync® the order form enclosed in this workbook.

Reading & Writing Companion   **71**

MEANINGFUL INTERACTIONS CA-CCSS: ELD.PI.8.1.Ex

Based on what you have read in the first two paragraphs of "Catherine's Calling," do you think she will do well as a Civil War nurse? Consider what you know about her skills and personality. Work in small groups to practice stating your opinion and offering helpful feedback to your peers, using the speaking frames. Then, use the self-assessment rubric to evaluate your participation in the discussion.

- In my opinion, Catherine will/will not do well as a nurse because . . .

- The text shows Catherine is . . . because she . . .

- Why do you think Catherine is . . . ?

- I think you said that . . .

- I think you made a good point that . . .

- I agree / don't agree that . . .

SELF-ASSESSMENT RUBRIC CA-CCSS: ELD.PI.8.1.Ex

	4 I did this well.	3 I did this pretty well.	2 I did this a little bit.	1 I did not do this.
I expressed my opinion clearly.				
I listened carefully to others' opinions.				
I offered useful feedback about other people's opinions.				
I was courteous when disagreeing with other people's opinions.				

REREAD

Reread paragraphs 3 and 4 of "Catherine's Calling." After you reread, complete the Using Language and Meaningful Interactions activities.

USING LANGUAGE   CA-CCSS: ELD.PI.8.12.a.Ex

Read each sentence from "Catherine's Calling" and note the bold word. Then complete the chart by filling in the correct synonyms and antonyms from the options.

Synonym			Antonym		
boomed	run away	near	stayed	far	whispered

Sentence	Synonym	Antonym
But she had never heard musket fire that sounded as **close** as her own heartbeat.		
Gunfire **thundered** around her.		
She had **fled** when the soldiers needed her most.		

Please note that excerpts and passages in the StudySync® library and this workbook are intended as touchstones to generate interest in an author's work. The excerpts and passages do not substitute for the reading of entire texts, and StudySync® strongly recommends that students seek out and purchase the whole literary or informational work in order to experience it as the author intended. Links to online resellers are available in our digital library. In addition, complete works may be ordered through an authorized reseller by filling out and returning to StudySync® the order form enclosed in this workbook.

Reading & Writing Companion   73

MEANINGFUL INTERACTIONS CA-CCSS: ELD.PI.8.12.a.Ex

Do you think Catherine should return to the field hospital or go home? What evidence from the text supports your opinion? Read the antonym pairs below and complete the chart by adding your own in the two empty spaces. Work in small groups to practice sharing and discussing your opinions, using the speaking frames. Use the word pairs in your answer.

brave	cowardly
helpful	hurtful
safe	dangerous
planned	
intelligent	

- I think Catherine is . . . and the field hospital is . . .

- The text describes Catherine/the war as . . .

- This evidence shows that . . .

- It would be . . . to return to the field hospital.

- My opinion is that Catherine should/not return to the field hospital. My opinion is based on . . .

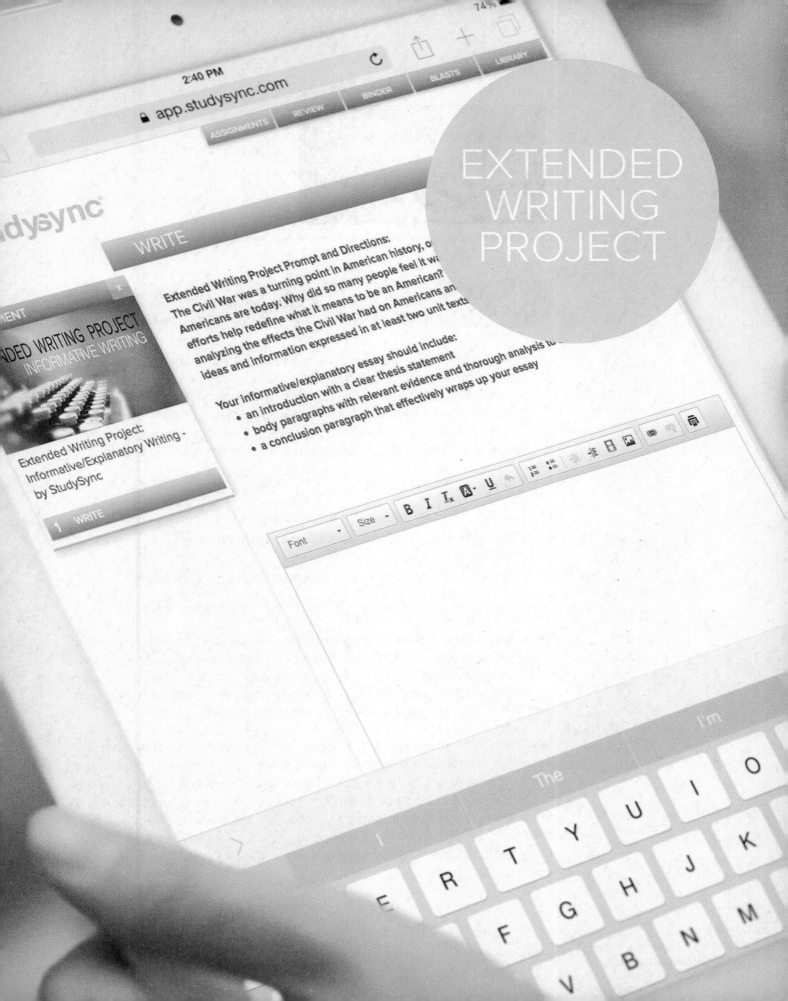

EXTENDED WRITING PROJECT

WRITE

Extended Writing Project Prompt and Directions:
The Civil War was a turning point in American history, o...
Americans are today. Why did so many people feel it wa...
efforts help redefine what it means to be an American?...
analyzing the effects the Civil War had on Americans an...
ideas and information expressed in at least two unit texts...

Your informative/explanatory essay should include:
- an introduction with a clear thesis statement
- body paragraphs with relevant evidence and thorough analysis to...
- a conclusion paragraph that effectively wraps up your essay

...NDED WRITING PROJECT
INFORMATIVE WRITING

Extended Writing Project:
Informative/Explanatory Writing -
by StudySync

1 WRITE

NOTES

EXTENDED WRITING PROJECT
INFORMATIVE WRITING

INFORMATIVE/ EXPLANATORY WRITING

WRITING PROMPT

The Civil War was a turning point in American history, one that helped define who Americans are today. Why did so many people feel it was necessary to fight? How did their efforts help redefine what it means to be an American? Write an informative essay analyzing how the Civil War changed Americans and their ideas about freedom. Use ideas and information expressed in at least two unit texts to reinforce your analysis.

Your essay should include:

- an introduction with a clear thesis statement
- body paragraphs with relevant evidence and thorough analysis to support your thesis
- a conclusion paragraph that effectively wraps up your essay

Informative/explanatory writing examines a topic and conveys ideas and information through comparisons, description, and explanation. The purpose of informative writing is to help readers expand their understanding of a topic. Informative writing examples include reports, newspaper or magazine articles, scientific studies, research papers, and non-fiction texts.

Well-crafted informative writing includes a main idea or thesis statement with supporting details, such as definitions, quotations, examples, and facts, that clarify and support the main idea. The informative piece has an obvious organization, such as cause and effect, sequence of events, or categories of information. Varied and strong transitions help the piece to flow and clarify the relationships between and among the ideas. Informative pieces draw an unbiased conclusion that is based on facts and logic rather than the author's opinion.

The features of informative/explanatory writing include:

- an introduction with a clear central idea or thesis statement
- details that support the central idea or thesis.
- a clear and logical organizational structure
- a formal style characterized by specific, precise language and domain-specific vocabulary
- citations of sources
- a concluding statement

During this extended writing project, you will be given more instructions and have opportunities to practice each of the elements of informative writing as you develop your own essay.

 STUDENT MODEL

As you prepare to create your own informative essay, start by reading this essay that one student wrote in response to the writing prompt. Examine this Student Model as you read, locating, highlighting, and making notes about each feature of informative writing that the student used.

The Meaning of Freedom

The Civil War was a turning point in American history that reshaped American ideas about freedom because it brought a resolution to the question of slavery. Prior to the Civil War, the issue of slavery divided Americans. Some were concerned that most African American people were kept as slaves. These people could not enjoy the freedom that white Americans took for granted. Others felt this situation was not only right, but also vital to the economy. This division was at the heart of the Civil War. Its resolution forever altered what it means to be an American. Many passages from the period explore these ideas of freedom. Abraham Lincoln's "Gettysburg Address" and *Narrative of the Life of Frederick Douglass, An American Slave* by Frederick Douglass are good examples. Both pieces discuss American views on freedom before and during the Civil War, as well as the necessity for change.

NOTES

In the excerpt from Douglass' memoir, *Narrative of the Life of Frederick Douglass, An American Slave*, he tells the story of how he learned to read in spite of being forbidden to do so. In fact, the idea of helping a slave learn to read in that time and place was so strictly forbidden that Douglass refrained from naming the young white boys he had befriended, and who shared their lessons with him. He said, ". . . for it is almost an unpardonable offence to teach slaves to read in this Christian country" (Douglass). To Douglass, the books he read "gave tongue to interesting thoughts" in his own soul (Douglass). The concerns of the white masters who had not allowed slaves to learn how to read came true. The books Douglass read gave him the words to express the truth that he had always felt: Slavery contradicted human rights on all levels. How could a country, said to be based on freedom, allow it? In fact it could not, because the contradiction made one part of the country stand against the other in war.

Almost 20 years after Douglass published his memoir, Abraham Lincoln gave a speech in the middle of the Civil War that said much the same thing and stirred much of the nation. Unlike Douglass, Lincoln did not have first-hand knowledge of slavery, and for him learning to read was not a forbidden activity. But he worked on the Mississippi river as a young man, and he saw the slave markets in New Orleans. He knew about the evils of slavery.

In "The Gettysburg Address," Lincoln acknowledged the same division that Douglass had written about. The Civil War had created a landscape on which fathers were fighting sons and brothers were fighting brothers. Families were torn apart and the nation was ripped in two. On one side stood the Abolitionists, who believed in freedom for all, and on the other side stood the slave-owners, who were in danger of losing their entire way of life. Those in favor of slavery were fighting to maintain the economic and social structure of America, and those against it were fighting for one of the strongest ideals upon which our country stands: freedom. Speaking to the crowd gathered at Gettysburg, Lincoln said that this nation was "dedicated to the proposition that all men are created equal" (Lincoln), and now was being tested to determine "whether that nation, or any nation so conceived and so dedicated, can long endure" (Lincoln). Mr. Lincoln acknowledged the need for all citizens to stand up and fight for this ideal.

In his speech, Lincoln called the movement toward freedom for all "the unfinished work" (Lincoln). He called on his countrymen to "be dedicated" in the fight for freedom. By the end of the Civil War, America was committed to the idea that "all men are created equal" (Lincoln). The country soon found, however, that some deep-seated beliefs about the nature of equality would take time to change, through many generations of Americans to follow. Healing got off to a slow start at the end of the Civil War. It is only now starting to come to fruition. Now we can see that the efforts of oppressed men like Douglass and brave leaders like Lincoln have redefined what it means to be a free American.

The Civil War forever changed our country's laws regarding freedom and rights for all. It took decades of legal and social changes to fulfill the promises made after that war. African-American people are no longer owned by others, but discrimination still abounds in many areas, compromising economic and social justice. African Americans are no longer held in iron chains by oppressors, but there is still work to be done in the arena of equalizing opportunity and just treatment. The work that our forefathers began with the Civil War continues to this day. It will continue until all persons, no matter what their race or circumstance, have the same freedoms everywhere in this country, forever.

 THINK QUESTIONS

1. What is the central idea of the first paragraph of this essay, and where does it appear? Support your answer with textual evidence.

2. How is the text in "The Meaning of Freedom" organized? Did the writer use a cause and effect, compare and contrast, or a chronological text structure? Cite textual evidence to support your answer.

3. How does the writer use relevant, well-chosen examples and quotations to show that Frederick Douglass' writing reflected the national division over slavery? Cite textual evidence to support your answer.

4. In considering the writing prompt, what resources, references or other sources could you use in developing your own informative essay? What ideas would you like to explore? List your ideas and discuss them with a partner.

5. Based on your background knowledge, texts you have read, and ideas you have studied, how would you answer the question, "How did the war between the states redefine America?" Write your ideas in a paragraph and share them with a partner.

Please note that excerpts and passages in the StudySync® library and this workbook are intended as touchstones to generate interest in an author's work. The excerpts and passages do not substitute for the reading of entire texts, and StudySync® strongly recommends that students seek out and purchase the whole literary or informational work in order to experience it as the author intended. Links to online resellers are available in our digital library. In addition, complete works may be ordered through an authorized reseller by filling out and returning to StudySync® the order form enclosed in this workbook.

Reading & Writing Companion   **79**

NOTES

PREWRITE

CA-CCSS: CA.RI.8.1, CA.RI.8.2, CA.RI.8.3, CA.W.8.5, CA.W.8.6, CA.W.8.9b, CA.W.8.10, CA.SL.8.1a

WRITING PROMPT

The Civil War was a turning point in American history, one that helped define who Americans are today. Why did so many people feel it was necessary to fight? How did their efforts help redefine what it means to be an American? Write an informative essay analyzing how the Civil War changed Americans and their ideas about freedom. Use ideas and information expressed in at least two unit texts to reinforce your analysis.

Your essay should include:

- an introduction with a clear thesis statement
- body paragraphs with relevant evidence and thorough analysis to support your thesis
- a conclusion paragraph that effectively wraps up your essay

In addition to studying techniques and methods authors use to present information, you have been reading and examining passages related to the way that the Civil War changed American ideas about freedom. Now you will use the new techniques you have been learning to begin work on your informative essay.

The topic of your informative essay will have to do with the effects the Civil War had on Americans and their ideas about freedom, so you'll want to think about how the people and events you've read about had an impact on the events that led up to the war, and helped to redefine the way Americans thought about freedom. Consider what you read in *Narrative of the Life of Frederick Douglass, An American Slave* and how it addresses the following questions:

- How have American ideas about freedom changed since the time before the Civil War?
- Why was it important for American citizens to clarify their ideas about freedom?
- Who was instrumental in discussing the problem and its solutions?

Make a list of your answers to these questions for *Narrative of the Life of Frederick Douglass, An American Slave* and at least two other texts in this unit, in order to develop an informative essay based on this writing prompt. As you read, look for patterns that begin to emerge. Are there any central ideas that surface again and again? What connects these ideas? Look for similarities in the answers you have noted. Do any ideas occur again and again? When you find these commonalities, you will be able to decide which texts to use in your essay. Use this model to help you get started with your own prewriting:

Text: *Narrative of the Life of Frederick Douglass, An American Slave*

Ideas About Freedom:
- As a child and slave, Douglass struggled with the idea that he would never be free like the white children he met, even upon reaching adulthood, and longed for an education.
- The white children consoled him with hopes that something would change that would allow him to be free.
- In voicing his concerns and frustrations, Douglass helped the white children to understand the unjustness of slavery and the differences between their freedom and his enslavement.

What Happened:
- Douglass bribed the white children to share their lessons with him, and he taught himself to read.
- This act of rebellion both freed and further enslaved him, as he learned more about the institution of slavery through books, and he discovered that slavery contradicted the country's foundation of freedom.
- This knowledge caused Douglass to feel more desperate than ever to be free, and his writings shed important light on the evolution of American freedoms from the Civil War era to the present.

After you have completed your prewriting, consider your thoughts and ideas as you work through the following Skills lessons to help you map out your analysis.

Please note that excerpts and passages in the StudySync® library and this workbook are intended as touchstones to generate interest in an author's work. The excerpts and passages do not substitute for the reading of entire texts, and StudySync® strongly recommends that students seek out and purchase the whole literary or informational work in order to experience it as the author intended. Links to online resellers are available in our digital library. In addition, complete works may be ordered through an authorized reseller by filling out and returning to StudySync® the order form enclosed in this workbook.

Reading & Writing Companion   **81**

SKILL: THESIS STATEMENT

DEFINE

The foundation of informative/explanatory writing is the **thesis statement**. This is a single sentence that summarizes the central idea or position that the writer will develop in the body of the essay through organized facts, details, quotations, definitions and other pieces of textual evidence. It also briefly introduces what the writer plans to say about the topic. The thesis statement most often appears as the last sentence of the introductory paragraph of an essay.

IDENTIFICATION AND APPLICATION

A good thesis statement:

- makes a clear statement about the central idea of the essay
- lets the reader know what to expect in the body of the essay
- is presented in the introductory paragraph
- responds completely to the writing prompt

MODEL

The following is the introductory paragraph from the Student Model essay "The Meaning of Freedom":

> *The Civil War was a turning point in American history that reshaped American ideas about freedom because it brought a resolution to the question of slavery.* Prior to the Civil War, the issue of slavery divided Americans. Some were concerned that most African American people were kept as slaves. These people could not enjoy the freedom that white Americans took for granted. Others felt this situation was not only right,

Copyright © BookheadEd Learning, LLC

but also vital to the economy. *This division was at the heart of the Civil War. Its resolution forever altered what it means to be an American.* Many passages from the period explore these ideas of freedom. Abraham Lincoln's "Gettysburg Address" and *Narrative of the Life of Frederick Douglass, An American Slave* by Frederick Douglass are good examples. Both pieces discuss American views on freedom before and during the Civil War, as well as the necessity for change.

Notice the bold-faced thesis statement. This student's thesis statement responds to the questions raised by the prompt and meets the requirements of an effective thesis statement. First, it reminds readers of the topic of the essay: that the Civil War was an important event in American history that changed Americans' views of slavery. Then it specifically states the writer's central or main idea about this topic: that the Civil War changed views of slavery by bringing resolution to a long outstanding question. A strong thesis will always have both of these two aspects, so when developing your own thesis continue to ask yourself these two questions:

- Have I clearly stated the topic of the essay?
- Have I clearly stated the central or main idea that I will explore in the body paragraphs to follow?

 PRACTICE

Write a thesis statement for your informative essay that articulates your central idea in relation to the essay prompt. When you are finished, trade with a partner and offer each other feedback. How clear was the writer's main point or idea? Is it obvious what this essay will focus on? Does it specifically address the prompt? Offer each other suggestions, and remember that they are most helpful when they are constructive.

SKILL:
ORGANIZE
INFORMATIVE
WRITING

 DEFINE

The purpose for writing an informative/explanatory text is to inform readers about a specific topic. To do this effectively, writers need to organize their ideas, facts, details, and other information in an organizational pattern, or text structure, that's easy to understand and that best suits their material.

For example, historians might use a sequential or a chronological structure, discussing events in the order they occurred. They may also employ a cause-and-effect text structure to show how one event can influence or cause another. Authors of scientific articles might choose a problem and solution text structure, which presents a problem or a series of problems and then offers or explains solutions on how to solve them. A social studies article that discusses immigration to the United States early in the twentieth century could use a compare and contrast text structure to compare these statistics to immigration today.

 IDENTIFICATION AND APPLICATION

- When selecting an organizational structure, writers must consider their purpose for writing. Often they ask themselves questions about the kind of information they are writing about. They might consider:
  › What is the main idea I'd like to convey to readers?
  › Would it make sense to present a series of events in sequential order?
  › Is there a problem with possible solutions?
  › What solutions seem likely answers to the problem?
  › Is there a natural cause and effect relationship in my information?
  › Can I compare and contrast different examples of my thesis statement?
  › Am I teaching readers how to do something?

- Writers often use words to alert readers to connections between details and hint at the organizational structure they are using. These words also act as transitions to create cohesion, or unity, and explain the relationships between ideas in the text:
  - › Sequential order: *first, next, then, finally, last, initially, ultimately*
  - › Cause and effect: *because, accordingly, as a result, effect, so*
  - › Compare and contrast: *like, unlike, also, both, similarly, although, while, but, however*
  - › Problem and Solution: *so, consequently, due to*
- Sometimes, authors may use more than one text structure or organizational pattern. For example, a text organized with information primarily presented in sequential order may also contain some cause-and-effect relationships in the text.
- Sometimes authors include headings to help organize the information in their texts into different sections.

 ## MODEL

The writer of the Student Model understood that by drawing on sources such as "The Gettysburg Address" and *Narrative of the Life of Frederick Douglass, An American Slave* he would be comparing and contrasting the feelings and ideas of two different figures in history.

In this sentence from the introductory paragraph of the Student Model, the writer makes the organizational structure clear:

> Abraham Lincoln's "Gettysburg Address" and *Narrative of the Life of Frederick Douglass, An American Slave* by Frederick Douglass are good examples. **Both** pieces discuss American views on freedom before and during the Civil War, as well as the necessity for change.

The writer uses the word "both" to identify something the two subjects, Douglass and Lincoln, have in common.

The writer of the Student Model informative essay, "The Meaning of Freedom," knew that he was comparing and contrasting crucial similarities and differences in the outlook of two famous historical figures. He used a two-column chart to organize his ideas during the prewriting process, color-coding the information so that it was clear what the figures had in common. What was unique to each individual is unmarked.

FREDERICK DOUGLASS	ABRAHAM LINCOLN
Former slave	President of the United States
Prevented from learning to read or attending school when a slave	Was able to learn to read
Wrote about the contradiction of a country based on freedom having slaves	Wrote about how the nation could not endure half-free and half-slave
Felt slavery contradicted human rights on all levels	Said that the nation was "dedicated to the proposition that all men are created equal and was being tested to determine "whether that nation, or any nation so conceived and so dedicated, can long endure."

PRACTICE

Using an *Organize Informative/Explanatory Writing Two-Column Chart* graphic organizer like the one you have just studied and/or the *Organize Informative/Explanatory Writing Three-Section Web* graphic organizer, fill in the details you gathered for at least two texts in the Prewrite stage of writing your essay. Exchange your organizer with a partner and offer each other feedback.

SKILL:
SUPPORTING
DETAILS

 DEFINE

In informative writing, writers develop their main idea with relevant information called **supporting details.** Relevant information can be any fact, definition, concrete detail, example, or quotation that is important to a reader's understanding of the topic and closely related to the thesis, or main idea. Supporting details can be found in a variety of places, but only those that provide substance for the thesis should be included:

- Facts important to understanding the topic
- Research related to the main idea or thesis
- Quotations from experts, eyewitnesses, or other source material
- Conclusions of scientific findings and studies
- Definitions from reference material

Writers can choose supporting details from many sources. Encyclopedias, research papers, newspaper articles, graphs, memoirs, biographies, criticism, documentaries, and online references can all provide relevant information for source material. Though information is plentiful and the source material varied, the writer must be careful to evaluate the quality of information to determine what information is most important and most closely related to the thesis. If the information doesn't support the topic or if the information doesn't strengthen the writer's point, it is not relevant.

 IDENTIFICATION AND APPLICATION

Step 1:

Review your thesis statement. To identify relevant supporting details, ask this question: What is my main idea about this topic? Here is the thesis statement of the Student Model, "The Meaning of Freedom":

> *The Civil War was a turning point in American history that reshaped American ideas about freedom because it brought a resolution to the question of slavery.*

Please note that excerpts and passages in the StudySync® library and this workbook are intended as touchstones to generate interest in an author's work. The excerpts and passages do not substitute for the reading of entire texts, and StudySync® strongly recommends that students seek out and purchase the whole literary or informational work in order to experience it as the author intended. Links to online resellers are available in our digital library. In addition, complete works may be ordered through an authorized reseller by filling out and returning to StudySync® the order form enclosed in this workbook.

Reading & Writing Companion   **87**

Step 2:

Ask what a reader needs to know about the topic in order to understand the main idea. What details will support your thesis? Consider how the writer of the Student Model follows the thesis statement with an explanation of *why* the Civil War was a pivotal moment in American history:

> *Prior to the Civil War, the issue of slavery divided Americans. Some were concerned that most African American people were kept as slaves. These people could not enjoy the freedom that white Americans took for granted. Others felt this situation was not only right, but also vital to the economy.*

But how has the Civil War reshaped American ideas about freedom? The writer provides more information to tie these details to the thesis statement:

> *This division was at the heart of the Civil War. Its resolution forever altered what it means to be an American.*

Step 3:

Search for facts, quotations, research, and the conclusions of others to help strengthen and support your thesis statement. As you search for details, carefully evaluate their relevance to your main idea. Ask yourself:

- Is this information necessary to the reader's understanding of the topic?
- Does this information help to develop and refine my key concept?
- Does this information relate closely to my thesis?
- Where can I find better evidence that will provide stronger support for my point?

 MODEL

In the following excerpt from Frederick Douglass's *Narrative of the Life of Frederick Douglass, An American Slave*, Douglass develops the idea that learning to read helped him understand important aspects of the institution of slavery that had been unclear to him before.

> I was now about twelve years old, and the thought of being a slave for life began to bear heavily upon my heart. Just about this time, I got hold of **a book entitled "The Columbian Orator."** Every opportunity I got, I used to read this book. Among much of other interesting matter, I found in it **a dialogue between a master and his slave.** The slave was represented as having run away from his master three times. The dialogue represented the conversation which took place between them,

when the slave was retaken the third time. In this dialogue, the whole argument in behalf of slavery was brought forward by the master, all of which was disposed of by the slave. The slave was made to say some very **smart** as well as **impressive** things in reply to his master — things which had the desired though unexpected effect; for **the conversation resulted in the voluntary emancipation of the slave on the part of the master.**

In the same book, I met with one of **Sheridan's mighty speeches** on and in behalf of Catholic emancipation. These were choice documents to me. I read them over and over again with unabated interest. They **gave tongue to interesting thoughts of my own soul,** which had frequently flashed through my mind, and died away for want of utterance. The moral which I gained from the dialogue was the power of truth over the conscience of even a slaveholder. **What I got from Sheridan was a bold denunciation of slavery, and a powerful vindication of human rights.**

In the first paragraph, Douglass reveals the source of his newfound knowledge: a book entitled "The Columbian Orator." He then provides details from the book to help the reader understand how learning to read helped him see important aspects of the institution of slavery. First, he describes reading "a dialogue between a master and his slave," in which the master argues for slavery and the slave argues against it. Douglass reveals that the details of the slave's argument against slavery were so "smart" and "impressive" that "the conversation resulted in the voluntary emancipation of the slave on the part of the master."

Next Douglass introduces another selection from "The Columbian Orator," a speech by Richard Sheridan. Douglass offers details about how these readings affected him and "gave tongue to interesting thoughts of my own soul," an enlightening process for Douglass. He then concludes by revealing the most important detail of all: "What I got from Sheridan was a bold denunciation of slavery, and a powerful vindication of human rights." With this concluding detail, Douglass shows how learning to read helped him understand important aspects of the institution of slavery that he had not fully understood before.

 PRACTICE

Review a text you plan to include in your informative/explanatory essay. Then choose a fact, definition, concrete detail, quotation, or other piece of information from the text that supports your thesis. Write three or four sentences that explain why this specific detail constitutes relevant evidence for your thesis.

NOTES

EXTENDED WRITING PROJECT
PLAN

PLAN

CA-CCSS: CA.W.8.2a, CA.W.8.2b, CA.W.8.5, CA.W.8.6, CA.W.8.10, CA.SL.8.1a

WRITING PROMPT

The Civil War was a turning point in American history, one that helped define who Americans are today. Why did so many people feel it was necessary to fight? How did their efforts help redefine what it means to be an American? Write an informative essay analyzing how the Civil War changed Americans and their ideas about freedom. Use ideas and information expressed in at least two unit texts to reinforce your analysis.

Your essay should include:

- an introduction with a clear thesis statement
- body paragraphs with relevant evidence and thorough analysis to support your thesis
- a conclusion paragraph that effectively wraps up your essay

In this step, you will apply the skills you learned in the Thesis Statement lesson, the Organize Informative Writing lesson, and the Supporting Details lesson. You will also consider what information best suits your purpose and the needs of your audience.

Begin by looking again at the information you gathered from the source texts. If you have not done so already, complete the *Organize Informative/Explanatory Writing Three-Section Web* graphic organizer to categorize your ideas into three groups and sort details according to the ideas they support. If you have already begun to fill in this organizer, expand upon the existing information. Be sure to find at least two supporting details for each idea. If there are missing details, return to your resource texts to find additional support. If you cannot find enough support, you may need to adjust some of your main ideas.

The organized information on the web that you created will guide you in crafting a thesis statement. Make your thesis statement broad enough to cover all three groups of ideas, but also narrow enough so your information

NOTES

addresses all of the points you want to make adequately. Remember that your thesis statement should clearly state not only the topic of your essay but also your stance on that topic.

The organized information and your thesis statement will allow you to create a roadmap for your essay. Consider the following questions as you develop your roadmap:

- What themes, patterns, or commonalities did you find in your survey of texts about changing ideas of freedom?
- Why is it important for American citizens to consider how our ideas of freedom have changed?
- How were the men and women who expressed these ideas instrumental in changing our understanding of freedom in America?
- What was the connection between the Civil War and our understanding of freedom?
- How do people who wrote about freedom both before and during the Civil War era speak to us in the present time?
- How are those changes apparent in our society today?

Use this model to get started with your road map:

Essay Road Map

Thesis statement:

    Introduction/Paragraph 1:
        Supporting Detail #1:
        Supporting Detail #2:

    Body/Paragraph 2 Topic:
        Supporting Detail #1:
        Supporting Detail #2:

    Body/Paragraph 3 Topic:
        Supporting Detail #1:
        Supporting Detail #2:

    Body/Paragraph 4 Topic:
        Supporting Detail #1:
        Supporting Detail #2:

    Conclusion/Paragraph 5:
        Restated supporting idea #1:
        Restated supporting idea #2:
        Restated supporting idea #3:
        Restated thesis or concluding statement:

SKILL:
INTRODUCTIONS

DEFINE

The **introduction** is the opening paragraph or section of a nonfiction text. In an informative/explanatory text, the introduction provides readers with important information by **introducing the topic** and **stating the thesis** that will be developed in the body of the text. A strong introduction also generates interest in the topic by engaging readers in an interesting or attentive way.

IDENTIFICATION AND APPLICATION

- In informative or explanatory writing, the introduction identifies the topic of the writing by stating what the text will be about.

- A writer may provide necessary background information about the topic in the introduction to help the reader understand the topic.

- The introduction also contains the main idea or **thesis** of the essay.

- An essay's introduction often contains a **"hook,"** or an element that grabs the reader's attention and piques reader curiosity to encourage the reader to keep reading. Examples of effective hooks include emotional language, open-ended questions, and surprising facts

MODEL

Look at the introduction of Abraham Lincoln's "Gettysburg Address" speech:

> Four score and seven years ago our fathers brought forth on this continent, **a new nation, conceived in Liberty, and dedicated to the proposition that all men are created equal.**

This introductory sentence of Lincoln's speech has several functions. First, it alerts readers to the topic Lincoln will discuss in his speech: America as "a new nation, conceived in Liberty, and dedicated to the proposition that all men are created equal." Second, this sentence also serves as the thesis for Lincoln's speech. Readers know that Lincoln believes that America is dedicated to the proposition that all men are created equal. Third, the opening line of the speech acts as a hook. Lincoln's use of emotion-laden words such as "conceived" and "dedicated" create interest and compel us to keep reading.

Because the first paragraph of the speech is only one sentence, the second paragraph provides more information about the main topic of the speech:

> Now **we are engaged in a great civil war,** testing whether that nation, or any nation so conceived and so dedicated, can long endure. We are met on a great battle-field of that war. We have come to dedicate a portion of that field, as a final resting place for those **who here gave their lives that that nation might live.** It is altogether fitting and proper that we should do this.

Here Lincoln has developed his main idea. Because the nation was conceived with these ideals, "we are engaged in a great civil war" and must honor the soldiers "who here gave their lives that that nation might live." Lincoln's thesis in this introduction might be summarized as follows: *We are fighting the Civil War to protect our ideals of liberty and equality for all, and we must honor the soldiers who have died fighting for this cause.* This important idea is designed to compel the audience's attention by creating a sense of patriotism, duty, and obligation.

 PRACTICE

Write an introduction for your essay that alerts readers to the topic, includes the thesis you have written and revised, and contains a hook to capture readers' interest. When you are finished, trade with a peer review partner and offer helpful and constructive feedback on your peer's introduction.

Please note that excerpts and passages in the StudySync® library and this workbook are intended as touchstones to generate interest in an author's work. The excerpts and passages do not substitute for the reading of entire texts, and StudySync® strongly recommends that students seek out and purchase the whole literary or informational work in order to experience it as the author intended. Links to online resellers are available in our digital library. In addition, complete works may be ordered through an authorized reseller by filling out and returning to StudySync® the order form enclosed in this workbook.

Reading & Writing Companion

93

SKILL: BODY
PARAGRAPHS
AND
TRANSITIONS

 DEFINE

Body paragraphs are the section of an essay that fall between the introductory and concluding paragraphs. This is where you support your thesis statement through analysis and by developing your main points with evidence from the text. Typically, each body paragraph focuses on one important idea to avoid confusing readers. The main point discussed in each body paragraph must support the thesis statement.

It's important to organize the paragraphs that make up the body of your text in such a way that the information is clear. Here is one strategy to use when structuring the body paragraph for an informational essay:

Topic sentence: The topic sentence is usually the first sentence of your introductory paragraph. It can also come at the end. It clearly states the main point of the paragraph. It's important that your topic sentence develop the main statement or point you made in your thesis statement.

Evidence #1: It's important to support your topic sentence with evidence. Evidence can be relevant facts, definitions, concrete details, quotations, or other information and examples.

Analysis/Explanation #1: After presenting evidence to support your topic sentence, you will need to analyze the evidence and explain how it supports your topic sentence and your thesis.

Evidence #2: Continue to develop your topic sentence with a second piece of evidence.

Analysis/Explanation #2: Analyze this second piece of evidence and explain how it supports your topic sentence and your thesis.

Concluding sentence: After presenting your evidence you need to wrap up your main idea and transition to the next paragraph in your concluding sentence.

Transitions are connecting words and phrases that explain and clarify the relationships among ideas in a text. Good transitions can connect paragraphs and turn choppy, disconnected writing into a complete whole. Instead of treating paragraphs as separate ideas, transitions can help readers

NOTES

understand how the information in two paragraphs works together, and builds to a larger point.

The key to writing good transitions is making connections between paragraphs. By making a reference in one paragraph to related material from a previous paragraph, writers can develop important points for their readers.

> **Example:** After escaping from slavery, Frederick Douglass became a leader of the abolitionist movement, and also a well-known speaker. There are other things to note about Frederick Douglass as well. Douglass also actively supported women's rights.

> **Revision:** After escaping from slavery, Frederick Douglass became a leader of the abolitionist movement, and also a well-known speaker. Though his stand against slavery is well known, however, his work on behalf of women's rights has received less notice from historians.

Authors of informative/explanatory texts use transitions to help readers make connections among ideas within and across sentences and paragraphs. Also, by adding transition words or phrases to the beginning or end of a paragraph, authors guide readers smoothly through the text.

Transitional words and phrases can also help authors make connections between words within a sentence. Conjunctions such as *and, or*, and *but* and prepositions such as *with, beyond,* and *inside* show the relationships between words. In this way, transitions can help readers understand how words fit together to make meaning.

 ## IDENTIFICATION AND APPLICATION

- Body paragraphs are the parts of an essay between the introductory and concluding paragraphs. The body paragraphs provide the evidence and analysis/explanation needed to support the thesis statement. Typically, writers develop one main idea per body paragraph.
  - › Topic sentences clearly state the main idea of a paragraph.
  - › Evidence consists of relevant facts, definitions, concrete details, quotations, or other information and examples.
  - › Analysis and explanation are needed to explain how the evidence supports the topic sentence.
  - › The conclusion sentence in each body paragraph wraps up the main point and transitions to the next body paragraph.
- Transitions are a necessary element of a successful piece of informative writing.

- Transitional words and phrases help readers understand the flow of ideas and concepts in a text. Some of the most useful transitions are words that indicate that the ideas in one paragraph are building on or adding to those in another:

To show:	Consider using transition words such as:
similarities	likewise, also, in the same way
compare and contrast	however, in spite of, on the other hand, on the contrary, yet, still, unlike, same, similarly
example	namely, to illustrate, for instance
added evidence	as well, besides, furthermore, moreover
sequence or time order	after, afterward, later, during, meanwhile, recently, first, next, then
cause and effect	therefore, because, so, accordingly, as a result
conclusion	briefly, on the whole, to sum up, finally

- The strongest transitions often restate the idea that you want to connect to the next idea.
- By the end of the essay, the reader should be able to look back on a clear path of support for the thesis statement that leads to the conclusion in the closing paragraph.

 MODEL

The Student Model uses a body paragraph structure to develop the main ideas presented in the thesis statement and transitions to help the reader understand the relationship between ideas in the text.

Read the body paragraphs from the Student Model essay "The Meaning of Freedom." Look closely at the structure and note the transition words in bold. Think about the purpose of the information presented. How do the transition words help you to connect the information presented in the essay?

Copyright © BookheadEd Learning, LLC

NOTES

In the excerpt from Douglass' memoir, *Narrative of the Life of Frederick Douglass, An American Slave*, he tells the story of how he learned to read in spite of being forbidden to do so. In fact, the idea of helping a slave learn to read in that time and place was so strictly forbidden that Douglass refrained from naming the young white boys he had befriended, and who shared their lessons with him. He said, ". . . for it is almost an unpardonable offence to teach slaves to read in this Christian country" (Douglass). To Douglass, the books he read "gave tongue to interesting thoughts" in his own soul (Douglass). The concerns of the white masters who had not allowed slaves to learn how to read came true. The books Douglass read gave him the words to express the truth that he had always felt: Slavery contradicted human rights on all levels. How could a country, said to be based on freedom, allow it? In fact it could not, because the contradiction made one part of the country stand against the other in war.

Almost 20 years after Douglass published his memoir, Abraham Lincoln gave a speech in the middle of the Civil War that said much the **same** thing and stirred much of the nation. **Unlike Douglass,** Lincoln did not have first-hand knowledge of slavery, and for him learning to read was not a forbidden activity. But he worked on the Mississippi river as a young man, and he saw the slave markets in New Orleans. He knew about the evils of slavery.

In "The Gettysburg Address," **Lincoln acknowledged the same division** that Douglass had written about. The Civil War had created a landscape on which fathers were fighting sons and brothers were fighting brothers. Families were torn apart and the nation was ripped in two. On one side stood the Abolitionists, who believed in freedom for all, and on the other side stood the slave-owners, who were in danger of losing their entire way of life. Those in favor of slavery were fighting to maintain the economic and social structure of America, and those against it were fighting for one of the strongest ideals upon which our country stands: freedom. Speaking to the crowd gathered at Gettysburg, Lincoln said that this nation was "dedicated to the proposition that all men are created equal" (Lincoln), and now was being tested to determine "whether that nation, or any nation so conceived and so dedicated, can long endure" (Lincoln). Mr. Lincoln acknowledged the need for all citizens to stand up and fight for this ideal.

In his speech, Lincoln called the movement toward freedom for all "the unfinished work" (Lincoln). He called on his countrymen to "be dedicated" in the fight for freedom. By the end of the Civil War, America was committed to the idea that "all men are created equal" (Lincoln). The country soon found, **however,** that changing some deep-seated beliefs about the nature of equality would take time to change, through many generations of Americans to follow. Healing got off to a slow start at the end of the Civil War. It is only now starting to come to fruition. Now we can see that the efforts of oppressed men like Douglass and brave leaders like Lincoln have redefined what it means to be a free American.

The Civil War forever changed our country's laws regarding freedom and rights for all. It took decades of legal and social changes to fulfill the promises made after that war. African-American people are no longer owned by others, but discrimination still abounds in many areas, compromising economic and social justice. African Americans are no longer held in iron chains by oppressors, but there is still work to be done in the arena of equalizing opportunity and just treatment. The work that our forefathers began with the Civil War continues to this day. It will continue until all persons, no matter what their race or circumstance, have the same freedoms everywhere in this country, forever.

The first paragraph in this excerpt from the Student Model begins by stating, "In the excerpt from Douglass' memoir, *Narrative of the Life of Frederick Douglass, An American Slave,* he tells the story of how he learned to read in spite of being forbidden to do so." This **topic sentence** clearly establishes the main idea this body paragraph will develop. The writer will attempt to show how Douglass taught himself how to read.

This topic sentence is immediately followed by details. The writer explains that Douglass learned to read from the white boys in his neighborhood, who "shared their lessons with him." The author then states that the books Douglass read gave him the words to express the truth that he had always felt: Slavery contradicted human rights on all levels.

NOTES

Directly after this, the writer opens the next paragraph with the phrase "Almost 20 years after Douglass published his memoir . . ." Then he provides information about Abraham Lincoln's speech at Gettysburg and how Lincoln's message was similar to Douglass's message even though his experience was different. The word "after" shows a transitional link between Douglass and Lincoln.

All three body paragraphs use **transitional words** to show relationships between the main points in each paragraph. Words like "however", "unlike", and "same" within the body paragraphs help guide the reader as they transition from one sentence to the next.

 PRACTICE

Write one body paragraph for your informative essay that follows the suggested format. When you are finished, trade with a partner and offer each other feedback. How effective is the topic sentence at stating the main point of the paragraph? How strong is the evidence used to support the topic sentence? Did the analysis thoroughly support the topic sentence? Offer each other suggestions, and remember that they are most helpful when they are constructive.

SKILL:
CONCLUSIONS

DEFINE

The **conclusion** is the final paragraph or section of a nonfiction text. In an informative/explanatory text, the conclusion brings the discussion of the topic to a close. A conclusion should reiterate the thesis statement and summarize the main ideas covered in the body of the text. Depending on the type of text, a conclusion might also include a recommendation or solution, a call to action, or an insightful or memorable statement. A conclusion should leave a lasting impression on a reader.

IDENTIFICATION AND APPLICATION

- An effective informative conclusion reinforces the thesis statement.
- An effective informative conclusion briefly reviews or summarizes the strongest supporting facts or details. This reminds readers of the most relevant information and evidence in the work.
- The conclusion leaves the reader with a final thought. In informative writing, this final thought may:
  › Answer a question posed by the introduction
  › Ask a question on which the reader can reflect
  › Ask the reader to take action on an issue
  › Convey a memorable or inspiring message
  › Spark curiosity and encourage readers to learn more

MODEL

In the concluding paragraph of the Student Model "The Meaning of Freedom," the writer reinforces the thesis statement, reminds the reader of relevant details, and ends with a concluding thought.

*The Civil War forever changed our country's laws regarding freedom and rights for all. It took **decades of legal and social changes to fulfill the promises made after that war.** African-American people are no longer owned by others, but **discrimination still abounds in many areas,** compromising economic and social justice. African Americans are no longer held in iron chains by oppressors, but **there is still work to be done in the arena of equalizing opportunity and just treatment.** The work that our forefathers began with the Civil War continues to this day. **It will continue until all persons, no matter what their race or circumstance, have the same freedoms everywhere in this country, forever.***

According to the thesis statement, the Civil War resulted in decades of changes to America's laws to ensure freedom and rights for all citizens. The writer then addresses the significance of these changes, which have resulted in freedom for African Americans. The writer also introduces two concluding ideas: "discrimination still abounds in many areas" and "there is still work to be done in the arena of equalizing opportunity and just treatment." These ideas emphasize the point that though the Civil War caused great change regarding the freedom of American citizens, there is still a need for further change to reach the goals of equalizing opportunity and fair treatment of all citizens.

Finally, the writer presents a concluding statement about the changes that began after the Civil War: "It will continue until all persons, no matter what their race or circumstance, have the same freedoms everywhere in this country, forever." With this final thought, the writer has presented an inspiring message and has created a strong conclusion for the claims made in this essay. Readers may be inspired to examine other texts from the Civil War era, to dig deeper into the issue of how the Civil War forever changed America's views on freedom.

 PRACTICE

Write a conclusion for your informative essay. When you are finished, trade with a partner and offer each other feedback. Use these questions as the basis of your peer review: How effectively did the writer restate the main points of the essay in the conclusion? What final thought did the writer leave you with, and how did this create a lasting impression? Offer each other suggestions, and remember that they are most helpful when they are constructive.

NOTES

DRAFT

CA-CCSS: CA.W.8.2a, CA.W.8.2b, CA.W.8.2c, CA.W.8.2f, CA.W.8.4, CA.W.8.5, CA.W.8.6, CA.W.8.10, CA.SL.8.1a, CA.SL.8.1c, CA.L.8.1a

WRITING PROMPT

The Civil War was a turning point in American history, one that helped define who Americans are today. Why did so many people feel it was necessary to fight? How did their efforts help redefine what it means to be an American? Write an informative essay analyzing how the Civil War changed Americans and their ideas about freedom. Use ideas and information expressed in at least two unit texts to reinforce your analysis.

Your essay should include:

- an introduction with a clear thesis statement
- body paragraphs with relevant evidence and thorough analysis to support your thesis
- a conclusion paragraph that effectively wraps up your essay

You have already completed several important steps for writing an informative essay. Most of the difficult work is done! Now use the information that you gathered during the Prewriting step. Combine it with the organizational structure that you worked out in the Plan step. Recall what you have learned about audience and purpose, an introduction that contains a thesis statement, body paragraphs with supporting details and transitions, and a conclusion that wraps up your essay, and you're ready to write the first draft of your essay.

Use your roadmap and other prewriting materials to help you as you write. Remember that informative/explanatory writing begins with an introduction and presents a clear thesis statement in the first paragraph. Body paragraphs develop the thesis statement with strong supporting ideas, details, quotations, and other relevant information drawn from the texts you have chosen. Transitional words between paragraphs and ideas help readers understand how different facts and events are related. They also help readers follow the information you

NOTES

present to a logical conclusion. Then the concluding paragraph restates or reinforces your thesis statement and leaves a lasting impression on your readers.

When drafting, ask yourself these questions:

- How can I improve my introductory paragraph to make it more appealing and grab readers' attention right away?

- What can I do to clarify my thesis statement?

- What textual evidence—including well-chosen facts, definitions, concrete details, quotations, and other information and examples—supports the thesis statement?

- Have all my sources been cited properly, both within the text of my essay and in a Works Cited page?

- Would more precise language or different details about my topic make the text more exciting and vivid?

- How well have I communicated how Americans changed their ideas about freedom?

- What final thought do I want to leave with my readers in my conclusion paragraph?

Before you submit your draft, read it over carefully for any spelling or grammatical errors. You also want to be sure that you've responded to all aspects of the prompt.

Please note that excerpts and passages in the StudySync® library and this workbook are intended as touchstones to generate interest in an author's work. The excerpts and passages do not substitute for the reading of entire texts, and StudySync® strongly recommends that students seek out and purchase the whole literary or informational work in order to experience it as the author intended. Links to online resellers are available in our digital library. In addition, complete works may be ordered through an authorized reseller by filling out and returning to StudySync® the order form enclosed in this workbook.

Reading & Writing Companion   **103**

REVISE

CA-CCSS: CA.W.8.2a, CA.W.8.2b, CA.W.8.2c, CA.W.8.2d, CA.W.8.2e, CA.W.8.2f, CA.W.8.4, CA.W.8.5, CA.W.8.6, CA.W.8.10, CA.SL.8.1a, CA.L.8.1b, CA.L.8.1d, CA.L.8.3a

WRITING PROMPT

The Civil War was a turning point in American history, one that helped define who Americans are today. Why did so many people feel it was necessary to fight? How did their efforts help redefine what it means to be an American? Write an informative essay analyzing how the Civil War changed Americans and their ideas about freedom. Use ideas and information expressed in at least two unit texts to reinforce your analysis.

Your essay should include:

- an introduction with a clear thesis statement
- body paragraphs with relevant evidence and thorough analysis to support your thesis
- a conclusion paragraph that effectively wraps up your essay

You have written the first draft of your informative essay and have received feedback on your work from at least two peers. The next step is to revise your draft to incorporate the suggestions and improvements you have been considering. Be sure to consider all that you have learned about constructing strong, logically organized introductions, body paragraphs, and conclusions that support thesis statements by providing evidence drawn from sources. Always keep your audience and purpose in mind.

Here are some ideas to consider as you revise:

- Review the suggestions you received from your peers.
- Focus on maintaining a formal style, which means your essay should be written in a serious tone. Your subject is important and your audience is reading the piece to fully understand the topic. Here are a few suggestions:
  › Review your piece for slang and remove any that you find.

> › Be sure the entire piece is written in the third person. If you find words such as "I," "me," or "mine," remove them. Also watch for addressing readers as "you." These words give your essay an informal, conversational feel which is not appropriate for an informative essay.
> › Read carefully to see if you accidentally included any personal opinions. Informative essays are unbiased. They provide information, but they do not try to influence or convince readers.

- Once you have revised for style, read your essay again and focus on the content and organization. How can it be improved?
  - › What details are missing to support your ideas? How can you clarify the development of America's ideas about freedom since the Civil War?
  - › Do you need to add any new textual evidence to fully support your thesis statement or engage the interest of readers?
  - › Think about the exact words you have used. Can you substitute a more vivid verb or a more specific noun to clarify a point?
  - › How can you strengthen the transitions to improve the flow of the essay? Make sure each transition correctly highlights the relationships between ideas.

- Evaluate your introduction, your thesis statement, and your conclusion. It is easy to edit parts of the body of your essay and to accidentally move away from your original idea as you do so. Be sure that any revisions do not move away from your thesis statement.

Please note that excerpts and passages in the StudySync® library and this workbook are intended as touchstones to generate interest in an author's work. The excerpts and passages do not substitute for the reading of entire texts, and StudySync® strongly recommends that students seek out and purchase the whole literary or informational work in order to experience it as the author intended. Links to online resellers are available in our digital library. In addition, complete works may be ordered through an authorized reseller by filling out and returning to StudySync® the order form enclosed in this workbook.

Reading & Writing Companion **105**

NOTES

SOURCES AND CITATIONS
sync•skills
Writing

SKILL: SOURCES AND CITATIONS

DEFINE

Sources are the documents and information that an author uses to research his or her writing. Some sources are **primary sources**. A primary source is a first-hand account of events by the individual who experienced them. Other sources are **secondary sources**. A secondary source analyzes and interprets primary sources. These sources are one or more steps removed from the actual event. Some secondary sources, however, may have pictures, quotations, or graphics from primary sources in them.

Reliable sources are those that are known to be accurate and trustworthy. Books and magazines that have been fact-checked, such as journals or encyclopedias, are considered reliable. Websites that are developed and maintained by a knowledgeable source, such as a university or the government, are also considered reliable. Today, however, it is possible for nearly anyone to develop a website or to publish a book without the benefit of others checking their work. Personal websites and information coming from the general public are not, usually, considered reliable sources.

Writers study their sources before writing to learn about the topic and the way in which others have treated it. However, it is not acceptable to take another person's ideas and call them your own. This would be plagiarism. Instead, give credit to the source where the idea or quotation came from using a **citation.** These are notes that give information about the sources an author used in his or her writing. Citations let readers know who originally came up with those words and ideas.

IDENTIFICATION AND APPLICATION

- Sources can be primary or secondary in nature. Primary sources are first-hand accounts, artifacts, or other original materials. Examples of primary sources include:
  › Letters or another correspondence

NOTES

> Photographs
> Official documents
> Diaries or journals
> Autobiographies or memoirs
> Eyewitness accounts and interviews
> Audio recordings and radio broadcasts
> Works of art
> Interviews

- Secondary sources are usually text. Some examples include:
  > Encyclopedia articles
  > Textbooks
  > Commentary or criticisms
  > Histories
  > Documentary films
  > News analyses

- Writers of informative/explanatory texts look for sources from experts in the topic they are writing about. When researching online, they look for URLs that contain ".gov" (government agencies), ".edu" (colleges and universities), and ".org" (museums and other non-profit organizations)

- A writer includes a citation to give credit to any source, whether primary or secondary, that is quoted word for word. There are several different ways to cite a source.
  > One way is to put the author's last name in parenthesis at the end of the sentence in which the quote appears. This is what the writer of the Student Model essay does after every quotation. For print sources, the author's name should be followed by the page number on which the text of the quotation appears.
  > Your citations can also appear as a list at the end of your essay. In the body of your essay, place a number after each reference to a primary or secondary source. At the back of your essay, list the numbers and identify the source that goes with each number.

- Citations are also necessary when a writer borrows ideas from another source, even if the writer paraphrases, or puts those ideas in his or her own words. Citations credit the source, but they also help readers discover where they can learn more.

 MODEL

In the introductory paragraph of the Student Model, "The Meaning of Freedom," the author introduces the sources that will be discussed in the essay:

Please note that excerpts and passages in the StudySync® library and this workbook are intended as touchstones to generate interest in an author's work. The excerpts and passages do not substitute for the reading of entire texts, and StudySync® strongly recommends that students seek out and purchase the whole literary or informational work in order to experience it as the author intended. Links to online resellers are available in our digital library. In addition, complete works may be ordered through an authorized reseller by filling out and returning to StudySync® the order form enclosed in this workbook.

Reading & Writing Companion **107**

NOTES

The Civil War was a turning point in American history that reshaped American ideas about freedom because it brought a resolution to the question of slavery. Prior to the Civil War, the issue of slavery divided Americans. Some were concerned that most African American people were kept as slaves. These people could not enjoy the freedom that white Americans took for granted. Others felt this situation was not only right, but also vital to the economy. This division was at the heart of the Civil War. Its resolution forever altered what it means to be an American. Many passages from the period explore these ideas of freedom. **Abraham Lincoln's "Gettysburg Address"** and ***Narrative of the Life of Frederick Douglass, An American Slave* by Frederick Douglass** are good examples. Both pieces discuss American views on freedom before and during the Civil War, as well as the necessity for change.

By listing these texts in the first paragraph, the student has explained to readers which two texts the essay will discuss.

In this second paragraph of the essay, the student has included direct quotations from the first text, *Narrative of the Life of Frederick Douglass, An American Slave*, to support his claim that this text discusses American views on freedom before and during the Civil War:

In **the excerpt from Douglass' memoir, *Narrative of the Life of Frederick Douglass, An American Slave*,** he tells the story of how he learned to read in spite of being forbidden to do so. In fact, the idea of helping a slave learn to read in that time and place was so strictly forbidden that Douglass refrained from naming the young white boys he had befriended, and who shared their lessons with him. He said, **". . . for it is almost an unpardonable offence to teach slaves to read in this Christian country"** (Douglass). To Douglass, the books he read **"gave tongue to interesting thoughts"** in his own soul **(Douglass)**. The concerns of the white masters who had not allowed slaves to learn how to read came true. The books Douglass read gave him the words to express the truth that he had always felt: Slavery contradicted human rights on all levels. How could a country, said to be based on freedom, allow it? In fact it could not, because the contradiction made one part of the country stand against the other in war.

Here, the introductory clause "In the excerpt from Douglass' memoir, *Narrative of the Life of Frederick Douglass, An American Slave*," lets readers know which text will be discussed in this paragraph. The student also gives credit to Douglass for his ideas by including parenthetical citations after the quoted material from the text: "He said, '. . . for it is almost an unpardonable offence to teach slaves to read in this Christian country' (Douglass)." A writer must always use quotation marks around words taken directly from a text. Note, too, that the writer uses ellipses to indicate where he omitted words in the original text. Writers sometimes omit less relevant words from quotations in order to be succinct. However, they must be careful not to omit words in such a way as to alter the original meaning of the material.

Including quotations and citations in an informative essay helps readers understand which ideas have originated with the writer, and which ideas belong to the author of the source material. Writers can also lend credibility to their claims by showing readers how information in reliable sources supports the writer's ideas.

The next step the writer of the Student Model must take to fully give credit for his sources is to provide full bibliographic information for *Narrative of the Life of Frederick Douglass, An American Slave* and "The Gettysburg Address" in a Works Cited page. This Works Cited page should appear at the end of the essay and include, for each work cited in the essay, the author's name, the title of the work, the place of publication, the publisher, and the date of publication. If the work is in a collection, sometimes the name of the editor will also be included. According to Modern Language Association (MLA) style, commas are used to set off elements within each of these general groupings, but each grouping ends with a period. If a source is electronic, the last element of the citation indicates that the item is from the "Web."

It is common practice to present the titles of full-length works such as books, plays, and movies in italics. Shorter works, such as titles of articles, chapters, speeches, short stories, poems, and songs are presented within quotation marks. When citing a speech, the writer must include the date on which the speech was given and where he or she found the speech. Consider the following example:

Lincoln, Abraham. "The Gettysburg Address." 19 November 1863. *The Collected Works of Abraham Lincoln.* Ed. Roy P. Basler. New Brunswick, NJ: Rutgers UP, 1955.

You will need to search online for each text you cite in your essay and gather its complete bibliographic information. Then use this information to create a Works Cited page to accompany your essay.

 PRACTICE

Write in-text citations for quoted information in your informative essay. When you are finished, trade with a partner and offer each other feedback. How successful was the writer in citing sources for the essay? Offer each other suggestions, and remember that they are most helpful when they are constructive.

NOTES

EDIT,
PROOFREAD,
AND PUBLISH

CA-CCSS: CA.W.8.2a, CA.W.8.2b, CA.W.8.2c, CA.W.8.2d, CA.W.8.2e, CA.W.8.2f, CA.W.8.4, CA.W.8.5, CA.W.8.6, CA.W.8.10, CA.SL.8.1a, CA.SL.8.1c, CA.L.8.1a, CA.L.8.1b, CA.L.8.1d, CA.L.8.2a, CA.L.8.2b, CA.L.8.2c, CA.L.8.3a

WRITING PROMPT

The Civil War was a turning point in American history, one that helped define who Americans are today. Why did so many people feel it was necessary to fight? How did their efforts help redefine what it means to be an American? Write an informative essay analyzing how the Civil War changed Americans and their ideas about freedom. Use ideas and information expressed in at least two unit texts to reinforce your analysis.

Your essay should include:

- an introduction with a clear thesis statement
- body paragraphs with relevant evidence and thorough analysis to support your thesis
- a conclusion paragraph that effectively wraps up your essay

Now that you have revised your informative/explanatory essay and received input from your peers on the revision, it's time to edit and proofread your essay in order to produce a final version. As you review your work, ask yourself the following questions:

- Does my essay follow the basic structure of an informative/explanatory essay (introduction, body paragraphs, conclusion)?
- Does my introduction grab the readers' attention in an interesting yet relevant way? Is my thesis statement part of my introduction as well as my conclusion? Does it respond to the prompt clearly and effectively?
- Have I included strong main ideas, supporting details, and relevant evidence to support my thesis and create a cohesive, vivid presentation of what I want to say?
- Have all of my sources been cited properly both within the body of my essay and in a Works Cited page at the end of my essay?

- Do I use appropriate and smooth transitions to connect ideas and details within paragraphs as well as between paragraphs?
- Have I presented my readers with a conclusion that summarizes my purpose and intent as well as coherently restates my thesis?
- Have I established a formal tone through the use of precise language and academic, domain-specific words?
- Have I incorporated all the valuable suggestions from my peers?

When you are satisfied with your work, move on to proofread it for errors. For example, check that you have used the correct punctuation for quotations, citations, and restrictive/nonrestrictive phrases and clauses. Have you used ellipses to indicate where in direct quotations you have omitted material? Have you used verbals correctly? Are commas used appropriately? Be sure to correct any misspelled words.

Once you have made all your corrections, you are ready to submit and publish your work. You can distribute your writing to family and friends, hang it on a bulletin board, or post it on your blog. If you publish online, create links to your sources and citations. That way, readers can follow-up on what they've learned from your essay and read more on their own. You might also consider using headings to organize your information or graphics to enhance readers' comprehension of your material.

Please note that excerpts and passages in the StudySync® library and this workbook are intended as touchstones to generate interest in an author's work. The excerpts and passages do not substitute for the reading of entire texts, and StudySync® strongly recommends that students seek out and purchase the whole literary or informational work in order to experience it as the author intended. Links to online resellers are available in our digital library. In addition, complete works may be ordered through an authorized reseller by filling out and returning to StudySync® the order form enclosed in this workbook.

Reading & Writing
Companion

111

Text Fulfillment Through StudySync

If you are interested in specific titles, please fill out the form below and we will check availability through our partners.

ORDER DETAILS

Date:

TITLE	AUTHOR	Paperback/ Hardcover	Specific Edition *If Applicable*	Quantity

SHIPPING INFORMATION

Contact:

Title:

School/District:

Address Line 1:

Address Line 2:

Zip or Postal Code:

Phone:

Mobile:

Email:

BILLING INFORMATION   ☐ SAME AS SHIPPING

Contact:

Title:

School/District:

Address Line 1:

Address Line 2:

Zip or Postal Code:

Phone:

Mobile:

Email:

PAYMENT INFORMATION

☐ CREDIT CARD

Name on Card:

Card Number: Expiration Date: Security Code:

☐ PO

Purchase Order Number:

StudySync Text Fulfillment, BookheadEd Learning, LLC
610 Daniel Young Drive | Sonoma, CA 95476